Geo. F. Hull

8 Oct '64

D1736272

BONSAI
FOR AMERICANS

BONSAI
FOR AMERICANS

*A Practical Guide to the Creation
and Care of Miniature Potted Trees*

Drawings by Florence Hull

By GEORGE F. HULL

DOUBLEDAY & COMPANY, INC.

GARDEN CITY, NEW YORK

1964

FIRST EDITION

LIBRARY OF CONGRESS CATALOG CARD NUMBER 64–11722
COPYRIGHT © 1964 BY GEORGE F. HULL
ALL RIGHTS RESERVED
PRINTED IN THE UNITED STATES OF AMERICA

TO

my wife, who always abets me in my enthusi-
asms; my daughter, who has lived uncomplain-
ingly most of her life in a house with more
foliage than furniture; my grandchildren, who
think everyone lives that way.

Contents

page

Introduction: "The Secret Wrapped in Mystery Enclosed by Confusion"   13

PART I   AN ORIENTAL ART ADAPTABLE TO AMERICAN WAYS

Chapter   1.   As the Japanese Practice It   22

Chapter   2.   Bonsai for Americans   31

Chapter   3.   Collections for Color   45

PART II   THE MATERIALS AT HAND

Chapter   4.   A Head Start with Older Plants   54

Chapter   5.   Collect Specimens from "Your Own Backyard"   68

Chapter   6.   Other Ways to Start Plants at Home—
Importing Bonsai   78

Chapter   7.   The Container as Frame   92

Chapter   8.   Moss, Rocks, and Accessories   99

PART III   ENJOYABLE RESULTS QUICKLY ACHIEVED

Chapter   9.   Guidelines   110

Chapter 10.   Step One, Step Two   126

Chapter 11.   Potting-Soil Mixtures   136

Chapter 12.   Potting: The First Transplanting   149

Chapter 13.   Training: Pruning and Wiring   158

Chapter 14.   Special Kinds of Bonsai   173

Chapter 15.   Variations in Treatment and Response   185

PART IV   CARE A SIMPLE ROUTINE

Chapter 16.   Keeping Them Small—and Healthy   202

Chapter 17.   Watering, Feeding, Root Pruning,
              Avoiding Pests   213

Chapter 18.   Adapting Bonsai to Your Home,
              Your Climate   226

REFERENCE

Glossary   243

Japanese Terms   245

Books on Bonsai   246

Index   247

Illustrations

(BY THE AUTHOR EXCEPT AS NOTED)

	page
Massive specimen of bonsai in azalea	17
Six-inch azalea	17
Photinia villosa, 24 inches	25
Zelkova, 16 inches	25
Miniature bonsai display *Sumiyoshi, Tokyo*	29
Exhibits of bonsai (3 ills.) *Sumiyoshi, Tokyo*	30
Demonstration of bonsai techniques *W. L. Widmayer*	34
Exhibit in California *W. L. Widmayer*	34
Course in bonsai at the Brooklyn Botanic Garden	35
Dr. George S. Avery, Jr., with a 40-year-old bonsai	36
Lath house *Arnold Arboretum*	37
Part of the Larz Anderson collection *Arnold Arboretum*	37
Miniature pine echoes larger trees	38
Thirteen-inch pine on the terrace	39
Grooming a blue atlas cedar	40
This juniper is 5 1/2 inches tall	40
Trees are a hobby on this window ledge	40
Training a young Hankow contorted willow (2 ills.)	42
Tree decorated with snow	43
Dwarf mandarin peach in a tub	44
Collection of bonsai prominently displayed	47
Small grove of pistachio trees	47
Eight-inch azalea	51
Young Red Jade crab apple	51
Blooming tropical malpighia	51
Reducing andromeda to bonsai proportions (4 ills.)	58–59
Demonstration of bonsai techniques (6 ills.)	60–63

Change in appearance of a dwarf Mugo pine (3 ills.)   64
Short-leaf pine growing from a crack in a boulder   69
Gnarled specimen of sparkleberry   70
Western species skillfully trained (2 ills.) *John Naka*   71
Ibota privet, an impressive specimen   72
New plants may be started from cuttings   81
Rooting stimulant encourages stronger development   82
Homemade propagating case   82
Steps in air layering (6 ills.)   86–87
The container is important in bonsai   92
Holes in pots assure drainage   94
Drainage holes are made easily in plastic   95
Planting an 8-inch larch on a rock (7 ills.)   102–105
Live oaks on the Atlantic Coast   111
Monterey cypress facing the Pacific   111
An oak in Tennessee   112
Trees with a common sculpturing   113
Bristlecone pine in the Rocky Mountains   114
Bald cypress in Florida   115
Wine-glass form of the American elm   116
Seventy-foot pine   118
Wind-swept trees   121
Sandblasted Engelmann's spruce   123
Developing bonsai in cotoneaster (4 ills.)   129–130
Developing bonsai in tamarisk (3 ills.)   131–132
Soil textures for bonsai pots (2 ills.)   140
Starting a small pond cypress on rock (5 ills.)   143–144
Plant tied to pot for stability   151
Metamorphosis achieved with nursery stock (3 ills.)   152–153
Inducing a new shallow-root system (5 ills.)   156–157
Low branches help develop a tapering trunk   164
Application of training wire (4 ills.)   165–166
Training wire can seriously injure bark   169
Remove wire in short lengths   170
Mame bonsai have a toylike quality   182
Four-inch quince bears a fruit   183

Tiny juniper planted in a hollow rock · 183
Stages in training a Siebold holly (4 ills.) · 190–191
Nursery-grown juniper to adapted bonsai (5 ills.) · 192–193
Japanese white pine, 40 years old · 204
Twenty-five-inch Chinese hackberry · 205
A record of 38 years (4 ills.) *Brooklyn Botanic Garden* · 206–207
Water applied in a forceful spray · 210
Root pruning, step by step (5 ills.) · 218–219
Repotting, step by step (5 ills.) · 220–221
Juniper, 16 inches · 227
Pinion pine, 38 inches *Don Jim, Hollywood* · 228
Hemlock, 7 inches · 229
Mistletoe fig, 5 inches · 230
Norfolk Island pine, 7 inches · 230
Maple grove, 25 inches · 232
Venerable specimen of trident maple · 237
Spruce bonsai decorates a terrace · 239
Larger pot lessens the hazard of drying · 240
Hardiest species enjoy winter outdoors · 241
Screen tempers the wind · 241

Drawings

(BY FLORENCE HULL EXCEPT AS NOTED)

Training sketch for dwarf Mugo pine *James R. Raker* · 64
Multilevel table for miniature bonsai · 107
Zelkova bonsai repeats form of American elm · 117
Formal upright style of bonsai · 119
Bonsai in wind-swept style · 122
Illusion of a battle-scarred veteran · 123
Training sketch for cotoneaster *James R. Raker* · 130
Tamarisk in nursery can · 131
Training sketch for nursery stock *James R. Raker* · 153

12   *Drawings*

Proportions create illusion of size (2 ills.)   159
Two trees make an interesting composition   174
Grove of trees   174
Rock may show entwining root structure   176
Groves surmount a rocky bluff   176
Cascade style of bonsai   180
Training sketch for Siebold holly *James R. Raker*   191

ACKNOWLEDGMENTS: for permission to print photographs previously published in *The Chattanooga Times, Plants & Gardens,* and *Popular Gardening;* for permission to use photographs made in the Brooklyn Botanic Garden

Introduction

"The Secret Wrapped in Mystery Enclosed by Confusion"

The art of bonsai, by which the Japanese grow miniature trees in containers, is stirring the imagination of Americans. Although this Chinese term adapted by the Japanese is often mispronounced and still occasionally misspelled, the word itself is coming into common use in our language, because there is no English equivalent that so neatly expresses in two syllables an idea unique in the field of growing plants.

Most Americans, however, who want to go beyond the definition must penetrate more than an Oriental mystery; the subject is beclouded by myths and nonsense, much of it of our own creation. Oversimplifications by practitioners can be misleading, exaggerations by admirers are often ridiculous, and sometimes even the experts in horticulture add to the confusion by their technically correct explanations of how plants are "stunted" or "dwarfed" in nature. (Bonsai are not "stunted" in the normal sense of being unhealthy, nor "dwarfed" in the sense of being misshapen or unnatural.)

The simple truth is that the care demanded by bonsai is not necessarily more mysterious than that required for many of our common houseplants. The techniques of training—although sometimes combined with consummate artistic skill to produce amazing results—are readily understandable. Only a few potting and pruning methods used by the Japanese are still not widely known here. For the most part, all techniques are easily understood, and are readily adaptable to the arts of plant culture as we know them.

The extent of the confusion was suggested a dozen years ago by questions I heard (some of them occurred to me, also, at that time), such as: Must you pay a high price or start 100 years ago in order to have a valuable plant? Can I get seeds of miniature trees? Is there a secret to growing bonsai? Is it worth ten dollars to get eight packets of tree seeds and information on how to start a business? Are bonsai houseplants? Do you starve them to keep them small? Isn't it cruel? Must they be watered several times a day? To all of these I have found the answer to be at least a qualified "no."

Today the same questions—as well as more searching ones—are voiced, and by more persons than ever, despite the greatly increased amount of instruction offered the public by bonsai clubs, arboretums, and other institutions and qualified individuals. Most of this recent information is sound. But too often there is not enough "exposure" for would-be growers to do more than spark interest. There is not sufficient follow-up to give a full picture of both the purpose of bonsai and the solution to practical problems. For most of us throughout the country, competent instruction is *not* near at hand, despite the fact that, in line with the awakening interest in many things Japanese, bonsai is attracting the attention of many more Americans who see in it possibilities adaptable to their homes.

A twofold need confronts those who would learn to grow bonsai or to adapt bonsai methods to other plants, if my experience is any indication: First, to distinguish fact from fancy; second, to gain practical information on training and care of bonsai in one's own part of the country, with plants and materials available.

Although all of us know the hazard of jumping to conclusions, the allure of a conclusion that seems logical is sometimes irresistible. Such false assumptions help spin the web of myths, which we dew with glowing generalities. Unraveling the skeins of fancy can, however, be as enjoyable as solving a mystery story—if we do not become discouraged by the false clues. Let us try.

It may seem a reasonable assumption that a bonsai specimen with proportions that suggest great age developed these characteristics while growing in a shallow container. The result can be that a beginner may nurse a tiny seedling in a minute pot in the hope that somehow it will develop a massive trunk; this offers a possibility, but not early likelihood. Or the beginner may assume that the root-pruning technique of repotting bonsai is what keeps a plant small—but that is not its purpose at all. We may decide that because a plant looks old, it must be old—myths about age are particularly appealing to man.

May we dwell on the matter of age a moment? In the case of bonsai, age sometimes attracts. The appearance of age in a diminutive plant, especially when reinforced by statistics, clearly arouses interest, even amazement. More than a score of years ago a Japanese bonsai expert, more ingenuous than many of the sophisticated writers of both West and East who have followed him, described a scene: "Those who had been admiring the beauty of the flowers or the fruit seen on some of the bonsai, but without finding anything particularly remarkable in them, suddenly began to show great interest when they were told how old some of them were. . . ."[1] Unfortunately, it is understandable that in the beginning the presentation of bonsai to the West was laden with references to age, as the one criterion the Occidental surely could understand.

In this area of fancy, I can report progress. Authoritative publications now rarely mention age unless it is of informative value or real historic interest. And in this country among bonsai growers the question "How old is it?" is considered as much amiss as for the first comment on a painting to be "How much did it cost?"

Elephants and bonsai, I think, have something in common, despite disparity of size—strange claims for longevity. Even a baby elephant, with his wrinkled mothproof hide, looks old, a fact that must have contributed to some of our romantic ideas about the age and habits of this animal. Some years ago the fable of age led one government to attempt to recover an elephant that would have had to be 150 years old to justify the claim. In part, this event led to an investigation which indicated that the average life of elephants is less than man's. No authentic records were found at the time of an elephant that had lived more than sixty-nine years, and careful check of known individuals disclosed that elephants usually show signs of senility in their fifties.[2]

Bonsai are not elephants, and I am not arguing for a blanket conclusion that plants never live to great age. Some specimens, natural trees, and a very few bonsai, have lived for centuries. But this is not the rule. That certain trees are possibly among the oldest living things on earth should not lead to the assumption that all trees live to great age. I think it is almost an understatement to say we commonly exaggerate the age of trees; we spin fairy tales

---

[1] Shinobu Nozaki, *Dwarf Trees*, Sanseido Co., Ltd., Tokyo, 1940.
[2] Richard Carrington, *Elephants*, New York: Basic Books, Inc., 1959.
Also: Longest credible life span of elephants is 77 years in contrast to 115 years for man, according to Alex Comfort, *Life Span Of Animals*, Scientific American, August, 1961.

on the subject,[3] somehow confusing the figures on the "oldest known specimen" with normal life expectancy. Add the age of the rare exceptions to our impatient observation of the slow early development of trees, and we may feel that trees live forever. Practical arborists know differently. They know that many trees planted in our cities in the early years of this century had become costly problems by the 1950s and 1960s, requiring treatment for weakness of age and expensive removal operations where they were overlarge or dying. Admittedly, the redwood trees are amazing heritages of the past, but even their life-span, for most individuals, is not measured in millennia. It is true that some forest trees are slow to mature, and that some historic trees have attained great age. These are the Methuselahs. But for many of our most popular shade and ornamental trees, the average life-span is much the same as for man. And there are popular kinds which regularly live a much shorter period. Although the life expectancy varies for species from north to south, and from favorable to unfavorable locations, most of the trees around our homes and in our cities are in the "prime of life" in their forties and fifties, with greatly prolonged life largely a matter of good luck.

As bonsai, species of plants can have about the same life-span as they would have in nature. Normally short-lived flowering and fruiting varieties still tend to be short-lived when grown in containers. Theoretically, a bonsai kept healthy and in small proportions (that is, freed from the hazards that come with great size) and given perfect care, could expect to live longer than a natural tree, although the unpredictable variable of man's devotion makes the prospect unlikely. In sum, the appearance of age in bonsai, as already implied here, has little to do with its actual age, which is not a matter of central concern.

---

[3] Harry Ashland Greene, "Historical Note on the Monterey Cypress at Cypress Point," in *Modroño*, Journal of the California Botanical Society, 1929: ". . . the tourist is regularly furnished with one or the other of the most wonderful stories of how and when the grove was planted by man. The age of the oldest trees is given to travelers as from 4000 to 8000 years . . . I am willing to believe that this most distorted of all trees . . . is 1000 years old, and that there are older ones in the grove. A tree sawn off at the ground . . . looks as if it might have lived 10,000 years; on counting its rings only 184 were found. I wanted to believe that there were cypresses in our grove at least as old as the Christian Era, but my conscience forced me to join the ranks of the conservatives . . . of course such persons are quite unpopular in this region."
C. W. Ferguson, Research Associate, Laboratory of Tree-Ring Research, University of Arizona: "Sometimes undocumented guesses are much more fascinating than are studied comments that can be ascribed to a source."

Figure 1

Contrary to popular opinion in this country, small bonsai seldom become large bonsai. If kept pruned and in a small container, for instance, there is little prospect that the 6-inch azalea shown in Figure 2 will ever become a massive specimen such as the azalea in Figure 1. As a general rule, bonsai with thick trucks and large, exposed root structures, Figure 1, are developed first in a ground bed or larger pot, or are large plants dug from the garden or country-side and adapted to life in a container.

Figure 2

THIS BOOK

The viewpoints basic to this book are these:

Bonsai are for your pleasure NOW, not a deferred value for future generations; perhaps a more lasting bequest to our grandchildren will be the greater understanding we develop for the beauty of trees, both in our home gardens and in the grand stretches of this nation. Enjoyment of plants treated in the bonsai manner is attainable immediately, in many cases; if a wide appreciation of the subtler qualities of bonsai is to develop, I think most of us must follow a pursuit and personal route to rewarding results in the beginning. When a bonsai dies, it is not necessarily proof that we do not have an Oriental green thumb; no matter how "timeless" a specimen may appear, it is a living plant and, as such, always is liable to death; sometimes the immediate causes of failure are unavoidable and as puzzling and difficult to diagnose as they frequently are in the loss of a large tree.

To allay the development of more false assumptions, I should make these explanations: This is not a book offering short cuts to masterpieces, although we will emphasize ways to achieve satisfying results in a minimum time. This is not a book debunking bonsai, although I hope it makes the techniques seem less formidable. This is not a book on the esthetics of bonsai, a subject on which I hope others, with better qualifications than mine, will write. Where esthetic judgments are made in this book, they should be recognized as limited in application and in no way suggesting the breadth of esthetic feeling and sentiment which bonsai can arouse.

To translate an art form, such as bonsai, from one culture to another, with full appreciation of all the esthetic, sentimental, historical, and religious elements that make it significant to another people, would be difficult, if not impossible. I make no attempt to do so. Here only is an effort to suggest guides to form and technique based on the Japanese model, to be developed by us within our own traditional love of nature and beauty.

And finally, this is not a book that includes all the techniques that can be used in the development and care of bonsai.

Within this book are described the techniques with which I have had personal experience in adapting plants and caring for bonsai. The methods are not difficult, and they are applicable both to bonsai and to the betterment of plants that are not bonsai at all; the distinction between the two is developed within the extent of my comprehension in the chapters that follow.

In large measure, then, this book is based first on personal experience, second on observation of the results of others, and third on a mountainous amount of correspondence with interested and informed persons in various parts of the country. To these bonsai hobbyists I owe a great debt, for opening their homes and gardens to me, for sharing their experiences. Of the hundreds of letters over several years, many, I suspect, would prove more interesting reading than the book they have encouraged. If there is faulty evaluation of information, I am to blame.

This book includes lists of native species and nursery plants adaptable for bonsai that indicate the range of supply at hand. I have made an effort to suggest ways to solve problems of the widely varying climatic zones of this country—not with pat answers, but by so pointing out some of the factors involved and relating the experiences of others, that a grower may be helped in arriving at his own solution. Illustrations include drawings (by my wife) and photographs of a number of outstanding bonsai and of other plants (largely my own) that are not bonsai but serve to show techniques or steps in development.

As to the author, perhaps I should explain that I have been inclined to be a skeptic since the teens, when I was alerted by the dictum, "Believe only half of what you see and nothing of what you hear." My skepticism was extended to the printed word some thirty-five years ago, when a wise managing editor told a cub reporter, "Never repeat anything you see in print until you verify it." This attitude has led me to an extraordinary number of mistakes and failures —and to some delightful discoveries. It kept me from believing that bonsai was as difficult as it sounded. I found that the fundamentals— and the fun—are within the grasp of anyone. Becoming a Rembrandt of bonsai is another matter, prudently left outside the scope of this book.

If there are exaggerations in this book, I hope they are confined to this INTRODUCTION, to the mystery that surrounds the subject. For my own unintentional oversimplifications and unwitting false assumptions, I ask indulgence of the experts. The creative artists in bonsai (and we have them in this country now), I am sure, are aware of the need for a broader base of understanding. Until more Americans know more about the mechanics of bonsai, it will continue to be what it is now, an esoteric art; the artists will remain unappreciated;

competent nurserymen who would sell bonsai will continue to require "references" before they can part with a truly fine specimen, because there is little future in a business that results in customers disappointed by their failure to keep a valuable plant alive.

My special thanks go to those who helped me find some of the answers: To Dr. George S. Avery, Jr., director, and to the staff of the Brooklyn Botanic Garden; to James R. Raker, who contributed ideas for training specific plants, in the form of sketches, which are included here in connection with photographs of plants at the beginning of their training; to patient librarians and the personnel of agricultural experiment stations and research laboratories, who have supplied me with accurate data; to Japanese experts, who have been most generous of their time; to bonsai clubs and regional bonsai organizations, in many areas, for their invaluable reports to me of local practices; to friends who served as eyes in Japan; to correspondents and friends throughout the country; to those who checked parts of this book but are not responsible for its shortcomings.

PART I

AN ORIENTAL ART ADAPTABLE
TO AMERICAN WAYS

Chapter 1

As the Japanese Practice It

Although the idea of potted miniature trees, as bonsai, seems to have evolved during the distant past centuries in Japan and China, the word itself came into use little more than a hundred years ago. Bonsai is, rather, pronounced "bone-sigh," with little accenting of syllable, certainly not to the degree common in English; if you listen closely you may hear a slight upward lilt to the trailing "e" sound in "sigh." Like all nouns in Japanese, it is both singular and plural, applicable to one plant or a dozen. The term became widely known as the plants themselves increased in popularity, and was coined to reflect the need of a changing concept.

Potted plants, including trees, have been grown in the Orient for time beyond record. Trees have an important place in Chinese and Japanese customs as seasonal and ceremonial decorations. In earlier times superstition colored their significance. The flower-apricot, for instance, was traditional at the lunar New Year's celebration. To bring this plant into bloom at the right season required, however, care that could be given more easily to potted plants. Such trees, kept in containers from year to year, had to be pruned to keep them productive and limited within practical size. This resulted in a kind of training that produced various forms, some of them unnatural and grotesque. The Chinese, for example, favored an "octopus" style for some kinds of trees, with branches trained like waving tentacles.

But the Japanese love of nature and naturalness reacted against such stylized treatment. One of the early records, sometimes cited in discussions of bonsai, is the comment of Kenko Yoshido in the beginning of the fourteenth century, "To appreciate and find pleasure in curiously curved potted trees is to love deformity."

Records of potted trees in Japan show the lineage certainly is old, and that it evolved from an even more ancient heritage in China. One of the first records of these plants may be found in the picture scrolls, dated 1310, illustrating the miraculous effects of prayers offered at a shrine in Nara. Then, in the fifteenth century, a famous *Noh* play shows the love the Japanese had for such trees as pine, apricot, and cherry, by emphasizing the obligation of hospitality felt toward a guest: an impoverished Samurai burns his favorite potted trees to warm a wayfarer, who turns out to be a member of royalty traveling incognito. The title of this play is *Hachi-no-Ki* (The Potted Trees). Bonsai is not mentioned by name.

Part of the awe inspired in Occidentals for bonsai comes from the truly ancient specimens that persist from these earlier periods. A five-needle pine belonging to Iemitsu, third Tokugawa Shogun (1584–1615), is said to have passed into the hands of an emperor and has been handed down to the present bearer of that title. There are pine and wisteria on display in the Imperial Garden and on the grounds of the Horticultural School, in Tokyo, with records that indicate they may be 500 years old. Such plants, of course, are not family heirlooms, but are extraordinary legacies preserved in the Imperial Household or under institutional conditions. And there is no sure indication that they were started and trained originally according to the present-day concept of bonsai.

There is no ancient written record of bonsai by name, but some believe the modern idea had roots about 125 years ago in the activities of nurserymen in the neighborhood of Azakusa Park, a suburb of Tokyo. At least the influence of these growers seems significant. They developed techniques for producing salable plants, which, in some cases, had the look of mature or old trees. And these plants were of distinctly miniature scale. By the second quarter of the nineteenth century, the park area was crowded with garden shops displaying apricot, cherry, and white pine in china pots, many with wavy branches tied with plant fibers in the Chinese octopus style. About 1880, according to one authority, a nurseryman produced Japanese red pines of a very small size; these were called *komono* (little thing) or *katatemochi* (that can be carried in one hand). With the breakdown of feudalism and the development of a wealthy merchant class, demand for these various nursery-grown plants became widespread. During his reign, the Emperor Meiji (1868–1912) encouraged bonsai as a national art.

The original impulse may have been to produce flowers for their beauty, or to decorate with plants for their superstitious meaning. With the passage of time, there were changes in styles, and evidently in purpose, although experts do not agree necessarily on how this came about, nor when. Nor does it matter. An evolution did occur. Whereas, in the olden time large plants, frequently stylized in the manner of the Chinese dooryard trees, were dominant, the favor swung strongly to very small plants. Perhaps imperceptibly at first, these came to represent natural trees in miniature. The shallow pots with their long horizontal lines contributed to the landscape effect. Later, especially after it was found that many wild species were adaptable, plants of a middle size were emphasized. With skillful care, trees that had been dwarfed by natural forces could be collected, transferred to these traylike containers, and in a relatively short time become truly ancient specimens that represented a bit of the beauty of nature beloved by the Japanese. Plant collectors were inspired to scour the countryside, from the mountains and the northern islands to Korea, seeking native junipers, spruce, and other trees with picturesque qualities.

What differentiated these plants from the many other popular kinds grown in pots? Magnificent morning-glories, of huge flower form and varied foliage, have always been distinctive of Japanese horticultural skill; chrysanthemums are grown in cascading opulence (sometimes in bonsai style); various ground orchids and *Rohdeas* enjoy continued popularity—all are potted plants.

But a new name was needed, and the present term came from the Japanese pronunciation of two Chinese characters, *p'en tsai,* meaning "tray culture" or "planted in a shallow container," though all bonsai are not necessarily planted in shallow containers.

In the eyes of the connoisseur, however, they all have one thing in common: *The art of bonsai lies not in what the plant is, but in what it suggests.* Other potted plants are grown for the beauty of their foliage, flowers, fruit, perhaps their rarity—their attractiveness as specimens. But bonsai is not merely a foot-tall plant, any more than a drawing is merely ink and paper. As with the artist's paint on canvas, bonsai evokes a response in the viewer, memories perhaps of a tree sculptured by the wind on the seacoast, a gnarled pine sturdily rooted to a mountain bluff, a stately giant in an open field, or a shady forest fragrant with the scents of spring, or filled with the rustle of autumn leaves.

The Japanese, inveterate tourists, take keen interest in visiting their public parks, shrines, and resorts. Japan is a land of picture-postcard scenes. Snowcapped Mount Fuji is seen in countless views, and one

The Japanese achieve the illusion of size in bonsai by skillfully adjusting the proportions of trunk, branches, roots and leaves.

Figure 3. Photinia villosa, 24 inches.   *Figure 4.* Zelkova, 16 inches.

visits mountain gorges, sheer precipices overlooking the ocean, and scroll-like vistas of the Inland Sea, with its islands, some of them the site of maple groves that turn to brilliant hues in the autumn. While the traditional Japanese perhaps will never again have the traditional occasion to travel long distances with his wife, he may well take his bride to some famous picturesque resort. And the modern Japanese traveler, like an American, is usually burdened with a camera: snapshots bring home the scenes, to preserve their nostalgic charm. But for the Japanese of both the older generation and the new, bonsai does the same thing, with subtle additional qualities.

Many trees and other woody plants are well suited to growing in miniature proportions. Some are found so in nature. Yeddo spruce, for instance, towers over 100 feet in parts of Japan, but on the tundra edges in the Kuriles, it is found measured in inches. Bristlecone pine, now rated as probably the world's oldest tree, may be seen in our Rocky Mountains diminished in stature as the growing site approaches the timberline. Battered and scarred by the elements, these trees yet thrive for centuries.

Trees indeed are the paragons of bonsai, dominant in size among living things in man's environment, and capable of long life. But impressive bonsai specimens, seen often in museumlike settings, should not obscure the essential quality of bonsai that may be found in lesser things. To the Japanese, the actual age does not count most, unless it combines with other qualities to arouse an emotional response in the viewer. Bamboo is especially loved, but it takes careful training and demands frequent and drastic repotting to maintain. Grace of scale may be achieved in it, though we may find little of the age-old quality of many woody plants. Other lesser plants also are bonsai in concept: a tiny tuft of wild grass, a small herb—even a stone may serve. All of these elements help rekindle the Japanese love of nature, the pleasure they remember from a walk in the country, or a trip to some place of natural beauty.

The Japanese do not have an exact name, covering all of these other forms related to bonsai, which separate them from the old-looking trees. Reference is made to herb bonsai, and sometimes these shorter-lived plants are referred to as simple, or quasi-bonsai, in search for an English word to convey their meaning. No comprehensive term, however, separates them from the tree type, which up to now is more clearly understood in the West. It seems best to say that there are several kinds of bonsai, some very long-lived, developed sometimes slowly over a period of years, others with much less life expectancy, but also greatly valued.

Short-lived bonsai, quickly produced and especially effective for seasonal display, are important. In the *tokonoma*, a kind of alcove in a Japanese home, a larger bonsai may be balanced with a lesser herb specimen beside a scroll hanging on the wall. Or an interesting rock may be put in the secondary spot. For summer enjoyment an aquatic plant, perhaps with an appropriate stone, may be used in a tray of water.

The *tokonoma* was originally a place for a religious shrine, but has become the main point of special care in the Japanese home. Here, in the simple recess, displays are arranged for certain occasions, or to honor a guest. The arrangement is usually changed at least once a month. Bonsai sometimes are also shown against a screen, at the entry, or on a verandah, singly or in groups. When not exhibited, they are kept in the garden outdoors, usually on benches.

Until the turn of this century, bonsai was practically unheard of outside the Orient, although Von Siebold, and others, with observations made as early as 1826, described them briefly as horticultural curiosities. In 1909 an exhibit in London astounded those attending.

But plants exported to the Western world, without the know-how to keep them healthy, always withered.

In Japan, popularity spread rapidly from the royalty and the Samurai to the merchants, and then to an even broader base in an industrialized society. In this century for the first time great public exhibits have been held, a notable one at the Art Gallery in Ueno Park, Tokyo, in 1927. Thereafter, annual displays were carried on from 1934 until the outbreak of World War II. One authority, Shinobu Nozaki, estimated that by 1940 there were a million bonsai plants in Japan.

Through the years the Japanese have developed many classifications for bonsai. By size, the largest ranges from twenty-six to forty inches in height, although this top measurement sometimes is violated. Medium is twelve to twenty-six inches, and is particularly popular because such a plant is not difficult to move, and is in good scale for display in the *tokonoma*. The small size, from seven to twelve inches, is easy to handle, and may be shown to advantage in many places, such as a desk. The smallest classification, a kind of miniature of miniatures, is under seven inches. These plants are called *mame*, meaning "little bean," literally (pronounced mah-may), and some of them range down to finger-tip proportions. Although they compose the class most difficult to maintain, growing them seems to be a special challenge. Large collections of them are to be found among bonsai hobbyists.

This by no means ends the classifications devised. No matter what size, bonsai may be further divided among those styled as formal upright, slanting, semicascade, and full cascade—plus many subdivisions. Beyond this they may be divided as to those with one or more trunks, a grove growing from a single root or from separate roots, wind-swept trees, trees clinging to rocks, etc. Classifications also are based on those qualities enjoyed—bare branches in winter, flowers or foliage in spring, autumn tints or fruit in the autumn. As this latter would indicate, many beloved bonsai have brief periods during the year when they are especially appreciated, and then they may lapse into a period of less attractiveness. Such could be the case of a tree in spring with delicate budding leaves that become too large in the summer for good scale, a specimen with massive trunk and root structure that is actually marred as bonsai by too-large flowers for a time in the spring, a weeping willow of seasonal grace that must be cut back to a stubby structure repeatedly through the years.

These classifications often mentioned by Japanese experts may bewilder the Occidental, or remind him of the complexities the uninitiated will find in our classes for flower exhibits, or in the divisions and point system for a dog show. But complexity is almost the only similarity. The Japanese, in their own country, do not as a rule exhibit bonsai in competition—any more than we would hold contests between the paintings of Picasso, Chagall, and Mondriaan. The terms they use are not for classes in competition, but are little more than names for kinds of bonsai. Often the same plant can be considered rightfully in more than one classification. These Japanese classifications are useful in indicating a kind of plant or style, and a study of them will increase understanding of traditional forms. The terminology is not, however, essential to your creation of bonsai.

The Japanese names for some of the classes of bonsai may be found in the glossary of this book.

Some fanciers have attempted to codify strict rules for bonsai styles, in much the same way as in *ikebana*, the Japanese art of flower arranging. Some plants, in fact, are mass produced, closely following a pattern. The idea of the triangle—the three points, heaven, man, and earth, so well known to modern flower arrangers—is much in evidence, but it is considered a guide to pleasing composition rather than a requirement.

Since the Japanese made this art their own, naturalness has been a prime criterion of bonsai, no matter how skillfully and artificially nature has been aided and speeded up by man. Perhaps in part this comes from the fact that bonsai are living plants, not cut flowers or branches. And collected wild specimens, especially valued for their character, often refuse to fall into any set style.

In general, the Japanese have less time for such an activity than we. And the hobby does require some daily attention. For that reason, many who take up interest in bonsai do so in later life, when they no longer work regularly. A retired businessman may have a yard full of small plants arranged on benches. Others fit the hobby in where they can. A speaker of the House of Peers collected a thousand specimens of *mame* bonsai, even carrying a few plants with him on trips in a special wicker basket, as one might a pet. An actor kept a collection outside the windows of his city apartment, returning home between afternoon performances to care for his plants.

Since 1947, bonsai has taken on the accouterments and organizations that, by title, sound much like any modern activity that wins the interest and allegiance of men. The Japan Bonsai Commercial Association holds exhibits on property owned by the Tokyo Bonsai Club, Ltd. There is a Japan Bonsai Trading Co., Ltd. There is a Young Men's Bonsai Association. There are many exhibits held each year, the ones in the big department stores being particularly heavily attended. There is a national magazine devoted to bonsai. A kind of "who's who" of notable living plants, *Bonsai—Photos of Now Famous Miniature Trees*, begun in 1957, is now in its seventh volume.

For the Japanese, bonsai are as easily come by as potted philodendrons, Easter lilies, or poinsettias are for us. Every department store carries bonsai and accessories. Prices there range from $3 to $300, or more. A survey showed that the big demand is in December, in anticipation of New Year; there is another increase in sales in spring and early summer. Dealers search the country for the pick of the current crop, or for old specimens, as one might for antiques. Japanese with bonsai find the kind of sifted soils favored for these plants readily available on the market. Experts will come to his door to trim and re-pot his bonsai, if he wishes others to perform these tasks. One may rent bonsai. One may even board one's bonsai at a nursery that specializes in this service.

Figure 5

A display of the smallest classification of bonsai. Each plant shown here is less than 7 inches tall.　　　　　　　　　　　　　SUMIYOSHI, TOKYO

Exhibits of bonsai are frequent and popular events in Japan. Those in department stores, such as shown in photographs here, attract many visitors.

SUMIYOSHI, TOKYO

Figure 6

Figure 7   Figure 8

Chapter 2

Bonsai for Americans

Unlike the Japanese in their homeland, most Americans cannot at this point in time go to the nearest department store to buy bonsai. In a few places in this country bonsai-trained plants are available in limited quantities, but for the country as a whole there are none to be found at all—or those that go under the name bear little resemblance to true bonsai. There remains the fascination felt by most of us who have seen well-grown plants or even photographs of them. The very living, individual quality that makes bonsai impractical as a standardized mail-order item is part of its special charm. When more and more of what we use comes packaged, molded, streamlined, precooked, and mass produced by automation, the charm of the unique and the handmade stands out. By acquiring just a little more information, I have found—it has been, I am sure, the experience of many others— that in bonsai there are reversals of our usual garden practices that arouse further interest: instead of feeding to produce the largest specimen in the least time, we learn to use a diet to maintain health; we restrain and direct growth, instead of always attempting to hasten it; we pot "down" into smaller containers, instead of "up" to push for greater size; instead of shearing twigs to create fat topiary specimens, we prune judiciously to reveal structure. For the gardener in suburbia overwhelmed by oversize shrubs, this would seem a way to have plants that would be companionable instead of competitive. To those of us who live amid the engulfing paved acres of megalopolis, a way is now open to bring a bit of nature into our lives.

But—and the questions loom large in our anxious time—do we have the time to grow bonsai? Have we the skill? Can Americans really find in it a useful purpose?

DO WE HAVE THE PATIENCE?

The answer is to be found in the comment of a gardener of Oriental ancestry who was quoted in a publication of the Brooklyn Botanic Garden: "Patience," said he, "is needed only by those who don't enjoy what they are doing. If one enjoys doing something, it doesn't require patience."

There are ways to apply the techniques of bonsai to growing plants with results that yield immediate pleasure. Longer-term projects are still of such foreseeable duration that there is satisfaction in the step-by-step process. Even in these cases the measurement of time is usually a matter of two, three, or four years, not decades. Extraordinary specimens, it is true, sometimes are the result of long years of patient training. But it is not always so. The normal process for the creation of bonsai requires less time than is generally supposed.

DO WE HAVE THE SKILL?

One who knows how to repot a geranium or how to prune a hybrid tea-rose bush already has the horticultural proficiency to qualify at bonsai; its techniques, of course, are not the same, but they are not necessarily more difficult. One who does not yet have the gardening skill at this level still need not find bonsai beyond reach, because basically what is needed is the awareness of the needs of living plants, and knowledge of the care required by the particular species in hand. It is not necessary (as it is not ever likely that anyone will) to know all about all kinds of bonsai. A cook or a backyard chef can earn a reputation without knowing all there is to know about the preparation of foods, from sherbets to shish kebab.

Those who have had a close view of the achievements of Japanese growers do not feel that we will add much if anything to the art. But we may eventually contribute to the techniques. Some of my correspondence shows that there are plant physiologists who, investigating the mysterious hormonelike growth regulators, believe these substances have real potentiality as aids in bonsai culture. Growth retardants in this class, which already have proved the ability in some instances to develop shorter internodes (leaves closer together on the stem) and shorter and thicker trunks, may prove of use. Control substances, on the other hand, that stimulate growth, could be of use during the period of training, to hasten development by breaking dormancy and making possible extra periods of growth within the annual cycle.

What is certain now, however, is that there are a number of modern gardening techniques and devices which can help simplify the care necessary for bonsai. In the ancient art of plant growing, what we call modern methods contribute only a measure of scientific assistance; some of them are of less than certain value. But certain of these methods can be helpful to many hobbyists (who, by definition, must keep their avocation secondary to a regular job) by reducing the amount and frequency of attention through the use of automatic devices, plastics, and other gardening methods well known to Americans. Where such techniques or devices might be of help, they will be described hereafter in this book.

DO AMERICANS HAVE A USE FOR BONSAI?

Rather than run the risk of mistaking personal enthusiasm for the wave of the future, I confine most of the following report to information on the present state of interest in the art of bonsai and on the effect the bonsai idea seems to be having on the culture of other plants and landscape design.

If a map of the fifty states were used to chart the interest made evident by bonsai organizations and by public reaction seen in attendance to exhibits, the large bright dots would be found on the West Coast, with concentrations in the San Francisco and Los Angeles areas, in Hawaii especially at Honolulu and Hilo, with a strong mark at Denver, Colorado, a scattering of dots in the mid-continent cities, and a number on the East Coast, with a special mark at New York City.

Some observers believe that the outstanding public exhibits of bonsai in this country are now attended by larger crowds than their counterparts in Japan, attracting as they do here not only those interested, but also the many who are curious about an art that seems mysterious and exotic. Huge crowds have gone through the turnstiles of the California Museum of Science and Industry, Exposition Park, Los Angeles, to see major exhibits. The same magnetism attracts the public to the show in the Hall of Flowers in San Francisco. Crowds have stood in line to see the "Japanese Art of Bonsai and Ikebana" in the lobby of a bank in Denver. In New York, Dr. George S. Avery, Jr., director of the Brooklyn Botanic Garden, has estimated that of the 1,500,000 visitors to that institution in one year, more than a million viewed the bonsai displays. The Brooklyn Botanic Garden, which has a large and varied collection of bonsai, has brought Japanese experts

Figure 9

A demonstration of bonsai techniques and part of an exhibit of bonsai in the
California Museum of Science and Industry, Exposition Park, Los Angeles.

Figure 10

to this country to give instruction in this art as part of its widespread educational program, and more than 2000 have "graduated" from various courses on the subject. In Boston, the Larz Anderson collection, at the Arnold Arboretum, includes some of the oldest specimens in the country. These have attracted much attention.

More public attention is focused on bonsai in those areas of the country where there are numerous bonsai clubs by virtue of the fact that now bonsai is listed in the premium books of state fairs and many county fairs. This has created some cleavage between newer clubs and traditionalists, who feel bonsai exhibits should not be competitions like the showings of livestock and canned fruits.

The uncharted areas of the country also have a degree of interest not so easily measured. In almost every section there are isolated individuals and small groups experimenting and learning on their own, doggedly seeking everything they can find written on bonsai, occasionally traveling considerable distances to pursue the subject. A few examples of the many within my limited knowledge include: an executive who exhibits plants he has trained himself in his offices in Manhattan, a retired businessman in New Orleans, an expert horticulturist in a small south Georgia town, a shipwelder in a Virginia

A few of the more than 2000 who have taken courses in bonsai at the Brooklyn Botanic Garden are shown here learning methods of potting, pruning, and wiring.

Figure 11

port. There are bonsai-trained plants thriving on a terrace of an estate on Long Island, in a window of a small basement apartment in the Bronx, in a corner of a yard protected from the southwest wind in Kansas, on plant benches in a converted chickenyard in Tennessee, on lanais overlooking the Pacific, on a patio with a view of pleasure craft on the coastal waters of the Atlantic. In one case, I know of bonsai that flourish under an automatic watering system that cools and refreshes plants twice a day during the hot, dry summers in the Central Valley in California. In another case, they are protected from the intense sub-zero winters in a deep insulated sun-pit in upper New York State.

In some places small groups of interested persons are formed who

Dr. George S. Avery, Jr., with a 40-year-old bonsai, one of the valuable specimens in the collection at the Brooklyn Botanic Garden. It is a Japanese white pine (P. parviflora) *trained in an informal style.*

Figure 12

neither get nor seek public notice. An example in New Jersey is a bonsai club, "a unique one—no rules, no by-laws, no officers, only members (4) and bonsai!" When my wife and I visited them, we found that each member used differing methods of potting, all successfully keeping plants alive and healthy. (The reader might remember this when he gets to Chapter 11.) Members of this group had

Figure 13
Some of the oldest bonsai in the United States are in the Larz Anderson collection at the Arnold Arboretum at Boston. The plants are displayed in summer in the lath house shown here.   COURTESY OF THE ARNOLD ARBORETUM

Figure 14

benefited from seeing the bonsai trees that grow in Brooklyn, and from getting instruction from experts.

Where exhibits of fine specimens and instruction are available, public interest has shown an accelerating increase in recent years. A justified assumption, I think, is that in this country the market is ready, the product (bonsai) is wanted, the only problem is distribution— not so much of plants themselves as of basic, practical information. So far the wide-spread sale of seedlings or "tiny tortured trees," without adequate information on purpose and care, has more often caused more disappointment than not.

The examples mentioned to this point are of bonsai in the sizes of the Japanese prototypes, trained more or less in traditional Japanese styles. There are, it must be made plain, many other ways of growing plants where the techniques of bonsai have found practical application, where insight from the bonsai concept has produced new ideas of beauty. Plant hobbyists have found bonsai methods of potting and pruning to keep specimens within manageable size, so that they can be enjoyed in areas far beyond their natural range. It is

In this country bonsai-trained plants are finding homes on terraces and patios and in the windows of city apartments.

Figure 15. A miniature pine echoes the form of larger trees.

doubtful that the tourist can adapt the Joshua tree to bonsai proportions, or keep it healthy outside of its natural desert home, but I have seen olive trees, with shapes remindful of old California specimens, in Pennsylvania. Small, portable plants can be given winter protection not practical for larger specimens, which makes it entirely possible to have a living giant redwood (pint-size version) in Maine. Winter-flowering apricots, once not uncommon in the Upper South until a few treacherous winters eliminated them from outdoor gardens, can be brought back to that area, and to places of much more severe cold, because as bonsai they can be protected from the early blooming time until the weather is more dependable in the spring.

Cold controls the northward limit of plants and, in some cases, lack of cold limits them southward. Thus, apples are not for subtropical zones, because there is not enough cold for the needed period of dormancy. I have not heard of an example, but in theory, at least, an orchardist from the North, living in retirement in south Florida, could enjoy the bloom of apple, crab apple, or pear, if he grew a healthy container plant to which he could give sixty days or so of artificially refrigerated winter. Variations in control are boundless.

Figure 16. A 13-inch pine displayed against natural setting.

Figure 17. Grooming a blue atlas cedar.

Figure 18. This juniper is 5 1/2 inches tall.

Figure 19. Trees are a hobby on this window ledge.

JANUARY
DECEMBER
27
FRIDAY

DECEMBER

Frau Pax

new code
513

3 4 3 8 8

Mr. Del Stockum
626 Forest Ave

Nihby Mr. Amarin

DECEMBER						
S	M	T	W	T	F	S
1	2	3	4	5	6	7
8	9	10	11	12	13	14
15	16	17	18	19	20	21
22	23	24	25	26	27	28
29	30	31				

1963

DECEMBER
27
FRIDAY

JANUARY						
S	M	T	W	T	F	S
			1	2	3	4
5	6	7	8	9	10	11
12	13	14	15	16	17	18
19	20	21	22	23	24	25
26	27	28	29	30	31	

Exotic plants can be the valued trophies both of travelers and of those adventurers whose explorations are confined to reading and correspondence. I have enjoyed one collection of a world traveler which included, among the many, an acacia from Australia, a jacaranda from South America, a silk oak from Queensland, tapioca from Brazil, poinciana from Madagascar, and a needled evergreen from South Africa too uncommon to have anything but a botanical name—*Widdringtonia Schwarzii*. The owner of these plants was in no way interested in training them with wire in the bonsai manner, but kept them in graceful proportions and small size by bonsai pruning and potting techniques. Many of these and other rarities she had grown from seed, the only form in which some kinds easily cross national boundaries.

One example will serve to indicate the romantic interest within this same collection. The plant was a specimen of bullhorn (a term applied to several American acacias), a tree with peculiarities enough to interest the most casual. The common name is earned by pairs of large, hollow spines which closely resemble the horns of an ox or buffalo. But the oddity does not end there: these horns are regularly used as the homes of certain ants as nesting places for rearing their young. They cut a hole on the lower side, where rain water will not enter. In addition to this housing, the ants find food in a peculiar waxy growth on the trees. Further, as early as 1570, Francisco Hernandez, sent from Spain to investigate the resources of Mexico, reported on the intense pain inflicted by the bite of these ants, which rush out and fall upon an intruder, if the trees are even lightly touched. Naturalists since then have concluded that, in return for food and housing, the ants serve the tree as a bodyguard of soldiers. On the northeastern seaboard, within the sight of the towers of Manhattan, I found a live botanical specimen of *Acacia cornigera* fully equipped with miniature bull horns—but without the ants!

Ripples from bonsai culture extend throughout America far outside the original concept. Houseplants and less common tropicals are trained and potted with new insight into the artistic proportions of plant and container, a subject that has been treated recently in many articles and at least one book. In landscape usage, further, the word "specimen" is taking on a new range; formerly it applied, in particular, to shrubs or trees of distinctive color or habit, such as the purple or weeping beech; now we find that a variety as common as Pfitzer juniper can be a striking specimen, if pruning is employed to reveal the angular trunks of old plants. Today, landscape architects often specify a "picturesque" tree or shrub, rather than the usual

Garden plants can be made more attractive by bonsai methods of training. Here the trunk of a young Hankow contorted willow (Salix Matsudana toruosa) was trained to a graceful curve. Figures 20, 21, to harmonize with the naturally twisting growth habit of branches and leaves of this plant. Figure 22 is the same tree two years later, growing in the garden, and decorated with snow.

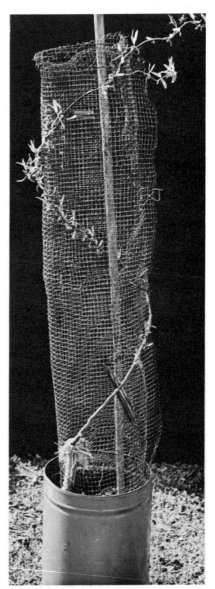

Figure 20   Figure 21

plump specimen, for courtyard or lobby of a large public building, as well as for the private homes of clients; the landscape contractor may search through the discard areas of many nurseries before the new specifications are met.

Line and form of specimens—qualities to be enjoyed the year around—often get more attention than flowers; training inspired by

Figure 22

bonsai is applied to such plants grown in containers or in the ground. Plants in containers are a new dimension in contemporary landscape design. The large containers do not demand the frequent attention of true bonsai; the plants usually are merely selected for interesting shapes that can be improved by pruning, though bonsai training by wiring and intensive pruning is not employed. Frequently gardeners and landscape architects, recognizing that these are not true bonsai, still give credit to their source of inspiration by calling them "adapted bonsai."

This picturesque dwarf mandarin peach, formerly grown in the ground, was made adaptable to life in a tub by bonsai methods of root pruning and training.

Figure 23

Chapter 3

Collections for Color

One quality of bonsai that is often overlooked is color. We are likely to remember as an outstanding example some weather-beaten juniper or twisted pine, an image in the mind of line and mass etched only in black and white. Earth-colored containers and natural tree forms combine to create a landscape effect that evokes memories and emotions, a subtle communication that the bonsai transmits from nature to the individual. Bright colors and startling shapes would, indeed, block that function by stopping attention at the plant itself; it would be like talking *to* the telephone instead of *through* it to the person on the other end of the line.

But this idea of monochrome can be carried too far. Color is part of nature; flowers were created to attract hummingbirds, insects—and man. There is no reason that those with an awakening interest in bonsai should neglect this attraction.

The Japanese especially value changes through the year that are suggested by color—the reds and yellow-greens of expanding buds in spring, the flowers and varied foliage shades of spring and summer, the indescribably beautiful hues of autumn, the brown or gray bare branches in winter. Bonsai play an important part in the home decorations used to mark the seasons. The point of color in an arrangement reminiscent of autumn could be a small persimmon with glowing fruit against the grayed background of the *tokonoma*, on which is hung a long scroll consisting of calligraphy or a picture in monochrome. Or the color might be provided by a maple bonsai with a few bright leaves scattered nearby.

Three bonsai sometimes compose a larger display, each on a separate stand in front of a plain screen, in the Japanese home. Among recommendations for seasonal display are these:

FOR WINTER: at left, a Japanese white flowering apricot; center, a pine; right, a yellow flowering adonis.

FOR SPRING: at left, a grass bonsai or sweetflag; center, a pink or white crab apple in bloom; right, an azalea with pink buds.

FOR SUMMER: at left, sweetflag or grass; center, a cedar or ginkgo; right, grass.

FOR AUTUMN: at left, a gentian in bloom; center, persimmon with ripe fruit; right, a spruce.

Another type of decoration to celebrate the season is a kind of tray landscape that includes a number of small plants. Such a miniature may be colorful by reason of the yellow flowers of winter aconite, bright berries of ardisia, and red winter foliage of nandina, or the "seven grasses of autumn" may be brightened by the purple of Chinese bellflower or the pink and white of bush clover.

It should be noted that in this traditional Japanese way of enjoying bonsai, the plants are not static items of decoration; they are brought to the center of the stage for a performance of a few days, then returned to an area more favorable for their growth. They are not rubber plants, nor philodendrons that gather dust as they grow too large. Bonsai used this way are akin to an arrangement of fresh flowers that no one expects to keep in place for more than a brief period. Unlike the flowers, the bonsai is not thrown away, but returns to its place in the growing area, a kind of "re-usable arrangement" that may increase in beauty through the years.

Although the Japanese use bonsai interchangeably with flower arrangements to some extent, and in American homes, often where flowers are used, bonsai also will find a proper setting, there are distinctions. The traditional Japanese home offers a simple background for flowers or bonsai; this is not always true in our homes. Truly fine specimens of bonsai are not well fitted to compete with bric-a-brac; they are not always capable (as flowers often are) of demanding attention despite distractions. Bonsai are not flower arrangements. If they are to be considered in the same light, it should be on a level that is distinctly *shibui*, a Japanese word not easily translated, but understood by some decorators in this country as that quality of restrained elegance, which demands a second look to be fully appreciated. In a sense, *shibui* is the reverse of "gaudy." The finer the bonsai, in other words, the more it deserves care in its presentation, an uncluttered setting with plain background and effective lighting—the elegance of simplicity.

However, all bonsai are not as subtle as these standards set by the

Figure 24

A collection of bonsai, Figure 24, offers an opportunity to display them in a place of prominence during the times when they are especially colorful. Figure 25 shows a small grove of pistachio trees (11 inches) whose foliage turns to brilliant orange-scarlet in autumn.

Figure 25

purists would suggest. Even Japanese connoisseurs grow some varieties of azaleas, as an example, that remain models of restraint for eleven months of the year, then don a Mardi gras cloak of brilliant color. For bloom in the true bonsai tradition, small flowers of delicate hues are appropriate; with this in mind, kinds with small blossoms (or fruit, if this is a feature) should be selected, for bonsai culture does not materially reduce the size of them.

But it is in this area of color that I think many beginners will find some of the early pleasures on the path toward bonsai. Developing an azalea of real bonsai stature might require a long search for a suitable old plant, and some skill and time in adapting it to the right container. On the other hand, enjoyment of azaleas in the training period can be immediate. And plants that are in no way true bonsai, but whose color and beauty are enhanced by adapting bonsai methods of potting, pruning, and training, are attainable almost instantly.

One good way, then, to start enjoying bonsai at the very beginning is to have a collection of plants, some of them selected for their colorful qualities. If you are going to have one bonsai-type plant, you might as well have several; there is very little increase in the attention required, but the possibility of increased pleasure is much greater. A single plant is likely either to become a dust-catching decorator's item, or an only child that gets more attention than is good for it.

A few examples of colorful plants that have been grown by hobbyists in this country will indicate some of the possibilities. One is flowering quince, a common shrub adapted to most areas, which is popular because its beautiful flowers stud the bare branches early in the year. Although old specimens respond well to drastic pruning of both top and roots, to train them as bonsai, the quicker route to a flowering plant is to select a younger one with interesting branch structure from the wide assortment of container-grown plants offered by nurserymen. The dwarf Japanese quince (*Chaenomeles japonica* varieties) is one of several kinds that often assume picturesque branching when quite small. In late winter such a plant may be repotted into something more attractive than the nursery pot, the root ball made more shallow for better proportions, excess and crossing branches pruned away and, perhaps, one or two wired to a different position for better composition. The plant is ready for an early spring show. As soon as buds indicate the start of growth, the plant should be brought to a cool place indoors and kept watered. After flowering, keep the plant in good light and away from hard frost until spring weather has moderated to the point where it is safe to put it outdoors.

Azaleas by nature have shallow, compact root systems that permit safe transplanting, even when they are in bloom, if reasonable care is exercised. (More detailed information on their selection, care, and training will be found in Chapter 15.) In some climate zones, brilliant early-flowering azaleas can prove to be more rewarding as potted plants than when growing in the garden. At our home, where spring weather often produces rapid changes from hot sun to driving rain to frost during some seasons outdoors, the early azaleas may prove to be attractive five days or fewer. Indoors we regularly expect to enjoy the potted ones for five weeks.

Japanese maples are another example of a species whose color may be quickly enjoyed in a container. These are very slow-growing trees that take a long time to achieve enough size in the garden to make them effective, unless a very high price is paid for an old specimen. Small container plants, on the other hand, can be displayed so their beauty may be seen at close range and enjoyed despite their size. Even young nursery plants, especially some of the thread- or fern-leaf variations (*Acer palmatum dissectum*) may be found that have developed picturesque forms. Spring foliage is colorful; some kinds remain red all summer, and most of them turn to beautiful shades of yellow, orange, and scarlet in autumn in climates where they are adapted.

A little plant hunting among the tropicals or subtropical species can be productive of colorful plants. One that I have seen well grown is pistachio (not the one that produces the edible nuts, but a Chinese relative sometimes grown in California and other mild climates). The compound leaves turn brilliant orange and red before they drop. Malpighia is a tender evergreen shrub with tiny hollylike leaves used in Florida gardens, sometimes as a hedge. Older pot plants soon develop interesting trunks and exposed-root systems.

A bonsai approach to potting and display also can bring new interest to commonplace plants. Dwarf geraniums that would never have been noticed in a conventional red clay pot become conversation pieces pruned and potted as bonsai. I have seen mistletoe fig (*Ficus diversifolia*), a kinsman of the rubber plant, trained as a graceful little specimen in a shallow bonsai pot, displaying bright diminutive "figs" over a long period. There is even potential for summer flowers in the popular bedding plant, lantana. This species actually is a long-lived tender shrub, which, in restrained size as a potted plant, can be kept for many years.

Traditional bonsai offer color interest throughout the season, especially effective because of the close view such plants make possible. At this intimate approach we see the tiny bundles of yellow-green leaves on larch, the "candles" of new growth on pine, the winged fruits of maple. Many common trees have lovely flowers that are overlooked on large specimens. How often do we enjoy the beauty of *flowers* and budding leaves on oak trees?

Some of the plants mentioned in this chapter will never achieve the treelike proportions of venerable bonsai, but I believe their inclusion in American collections, for those who find them attractive, is justified in the same way that expert Japanese fanciers often show their sentimental attachment to some ornamental species, such as the fragrant fingered citron or specimens of *Rohdeas*. The *Rohdeas* are a kind of plant with long straplike leaves, inconspicuous flowers, and a berrylike fruit. The favor shown them by Japanese growers has resulted in the development of scores of varieties; specimen plants bring high prices. Neither the fingered citron (*Citrus medica*) nor the *Rohdeas* achieve a tree form, but are often included in the collections of bonsai fanciers.

COLOR BY SEASONS

Brief lists of some plants offering color through the seasons follow. It should be noted by beginners that some popular fruit trees are listed, and that these are difficult to control and bring into bloom because they must produce new branches or twigs for a crop of flower buds, thus involving a more complex kind of pruning. These kinds are more easily handled as large tubbed plants.

SPRING:
Azalea, flowering quince, redbud, crab apple, peach, pear, maple, red-leaf barberry, Prunus "Hally Jolivette."

SUMMER:
Pomegranate, malpighia (*M. coccigera*), lantana, crape myrtle, red-leaf barberry.

AUTUMN:
Foliage color – Maple, ginkgo, cotoneaster, hornbeam, hawthorn, pistachio, some azaleas, sumach, crape myrtle, barberry, sweet gum.
Berries – Fire thorn (*pyracantha*), cotoneaster, hawthorn, bittersweet.

Flowers, foliage, and fruit of small
plants can be enjoyed at close
range when they are grown in bonsai
pots. The azalea (8 inches) in
Figure 26 has colorful foliage in fall
and winter, bright flowers in
early spring. The young Red Jade
crab apple (9 inches) in Figure 27
blooms in spring, bears tiny
crab apples in the autumn months.
The tropical malpighia (M.
coccigera—6 inches), Figure 28,
blooms repeatedly in summer.

Figure 26

Figure 27

Figure 28

Flowers – *Camellia sasanqua* and *C. hiemalis* varieties (especially Shishi-gashira, Bonsai Baby, and Elfin Rose).

Lists of nursery plants and native species appended to the next two chapters include a number of varieties which also are colorful at times.

PART II
THE MATERIALS AT HAND

Chapter 4

A Head Start with Older Plants

Purchase of a completely trained bonsai is not necessarily the most desirable route to entry into the so far rather exclusive coterie of bonsai owners. Although there are distinct differences, buying an original painting and a "finished" bonsai are somewhat similar undertakings in this country, with many overtones the same. Prices, except for the works of the most famous painters, in the two fields are in the same range. A few nurseries, like galleries, have outstanding specimens in addition to other plants from good to not so good quality. In the top category, bonsai can command as high as $7000. In this country, on the East Coast, a nursery headed by a recognized Japanese authority has tagged plants at $3500. In Colorado, a plant has been offered for sale for $2750. An informant in Hawaii writes me that prices of plants available there range up to $1000. A West Coast correspondent points out that the very finest bonsai (like the finer paintings) are in private collections and rarely are on the market. There are, of course, some plants of good quality for sale at modest prices, but those in the lowest price category are little more than plants suitable for training. In fact, a number of reliable nurseries offer plants selected for bonsai, and a few have them partially trained. Finally, it should be said frankly, there have been many plants on the market described as bonsai that, by no stretch of the imagination, fall into this class.

Prices of good bonsai need not discourage those who become interested in this subject, because the place to start is not with a "masterpiece," in my opinion, even if you have the money to invest. Bonsai are distinctly different from other objects of art in that as living things they have a fourth dimension—time. A bonsai is not a static, completed work like a painting. The essence of bonsai is that it is alive, recording the change in seasons, growing, often evolving through training toward a more nearly perfect form. Even a finished bonsai must have care and some continued training, or it will deteriorate. Creating one's own is an interesting and instructive exercise that will give more pleasure in the possession of an outstanding specimen through the insight gained into the processes that produce the results.

There are many ways to start bonsai, but the one most frequently followed by advanced grower and beginner alike in this country is to adapt older plants that have already achieved some of the desired characteristics. For most of us, these are readily available from two main sources: (1) Nursery-grown plants in a wide range of varieties for sale at garden centers, supermarkets, greenhouse-plant specialists, and nurseries. (2) Plants you may dig from your own garden or from the countryside. Plants from these major sources are discussed in this and the following chapter.

Creating bonsai can be undertaken with little or no expenditure of money. Basic tools and supplies are present in the average household, or can be obtained at nearby stores.

In addition to the more rapid way of training older plants, the hobbyist may find use eventually for other common methods of plant propagation at home. These are described in Chapter 6. In regard to plants started at home, here are factors to consider:

SEEDS take the most time and patience to produce worthwhile plants, although there are some exceptions, and seeds may be the only way to possess some unusual species. Even experts find shrub and tree seeds unpredictable at times.

CUTTINGS require from a few weeks to a year or more to become well-rooted small plants. Some species cannot be started from cuttings. Others, however, are so easy and demand so little attention that almost everyone will enjoy this method of obtaining new plants, even if they are only prunings from older bonsai.

LAYERING is a technique for developing new roots on part of an older plant before it is severed from the parent. It is neither very fast nor entirely dependable, but there is a new twist to one method called air layering, an ancient Chinese practice brought up-to-date and greatly simplified by the use of plastics and plant hormones.

GRAFTING requires exact timing and considerable skill to be successful. Presentable results rarely develop in less than two or three years.

PLANTS FOR A START

Older plants that are readily adapted to bonsai training are to be found among selections from nursery-grown stock. These plants as a class are easy to convert because, in most cases, the root systems were especially developed to make transplanting practical. A wide range of kinds, both native and exotics from all over the world, are available. These stocks of woody vines, shrubs, and trees are sold in several forms:

BARE-ROOT describes how some varieties of deciduous shade, fruit, and ornamental trees and shrubs are handled during the dormant season. There is no soil around the roots, although the roots must be kept moist until replanted. Not many in this offering are easily adapted to bonsai use, although there are possibilities. Small seedlings sometimes found for sale are a gain in time over the process of sowing seeds yourself.

BALLED-AND-BURLAPPED is the treatment given many needle and broadleaf evergreens and some difficult-to-transplant specimens. The plants are grown in the field, dug with soil around the roots, and the ball of roots and earth wrapped in burlap. Selections from this class may be potentially very fine bonsai, and because most of the root system is preserved, the life of the plant is not in much danger even in the hands of the beginner.

COLLECTED plants is a term used by nurserymen to describe plants that have been dug from the wild. While not nursery-grown like the others, such plants—either bare-root or with some soil around the roots—are handled by a number of nurseries that specialize in native species. Probably most bonsai hobbyists will want to do their own collecting. Procedures are described in the next chapter.

CONTAINER-GROWN plants now are produced in this country literally by the millions. Retail dealers like them because they can be handled without loss over a long season. The entire root system is preserved, and plants are already accustomed to pot culture, so this kind of nursery stock is the easiest and safest to handle. Small- to fairly large-size plants are grown in quart, gallon, three-gallon, and larger cans or other containers.

Most small-container plants, especially in the big production areas with a long growing season in the South and Southwest, are brought to salable size in one or two years. Starting with rooted cuttings or seedlings potted early, the nurserymen feed and water these plants for maximum growth. Larger plants, which require more time in containers or in the field, often are cut back or pruned to make them develop into compact specimens. In both cases fat, bushy plants normally are the end product.

Although little that suggests bonsai is easily seen in such plants, the collector may discern under the foliage the placement of branches or the curving lines of trunk that are wanted in the ultimate bonsai. Points to consider when selecting plants at this stage are suggested in Chapter 9.

Perhaps the better way to illustrate how selected nursery plants may be started in training as bonsai would be to describe a specific example. Photographs in this book, Figures 29, 30, and 31, show three stages in the pruning and potting of such a plant. Figure 32 is the same plant after ten months. Within two years, under continued training, this should be a bonsai of considerable attractiveness. These pictures were made of a demonstration for a beginners' class at the Brooklyn Botanic Garden by Frank Okamura, a member of the staff there.

The plant used in the demonstration was a broadleaf evergreen commonly called Japanese andromeda (*Pieris japonica*) which is characterized by new red foliage in spring, drooping flower clusters in summer, and similar seed capsules in autumn. The four-foot, balled-and-burlapped nursery plant Okamura estimated at perhaps ten to fifteen years old. Within an hour he had reduced the size by more than half, and increased the natural grace of the plant by pruning to reveal structural lines, thus starting it on the initial stage of its career as bonsai.

The first step taken by Okamura was to remove the burlap covering on the root ball, and then carefully to dig away the soil at the top to show the spread of the trunk at the base and to expose any large roots that might contribute to an impression of age and size. The root ball was further reduced from the bottom, the lower roots pruned, and the plant potted (Chapter 12).

To facilitate study of the plant, it was placed on a Lazy Susan on which it could be turned readily. The curving trunk, the exposed roots, and the branching were taken into account in making a decision as to which side should be the front, the one shown when on display. Practically all of the current year's growth was removed by

A *four-foot nursery-grown Japanese andromeda* (Pieris japonica) *is reduced to bonsai proportions by pruning, wiring, and repotting in a one-hour demonstration at the Brooklyn Botanic Garden in February.* (Figures 29, 30, 31.)

Figure 29

Figure 30

Figure 31

Figure 32. November of the same year.

pruning, with special emphasis on eliminating the tall vigorous sprouts that maintained a fairly large diameter almost to the top of the plant. Then the remaining branches were pruned to create informal balance, show the trunk, and establish scale from the massive trunk through the larger branches to the smallest twiggage at the extremities. Finally, Okamura used some wiring (Chapter 13) to shape branches and to fill in the composition. The results at the end of the demonstration were not claimed to be an example of a finished bonsai, and, in fact, another plant might have produced a better result. But the example illustrates the basic steps. Figures 33 through 38 show another demonstration given by Okamura of these preliminary steps in adapting a nursery-grown plant, in this case a dwarf Japanese holly, to bonsai culture.

Preliminary steps in training a dwarf Japanese holly (Ilex crenata).

Figure 33. "First remove the burlap . . ."

Figure 34
"Branches suggest
best side for front . . ."

Figure 35
"Now, drastic pruning . . ."

Figure 36
"The lines are
here . . ."

Figure 37
"Some wiring will
help . . ."

Figure 38. "It begins to take shape . . ."

Another step-by-step example is shown in Figures 39, 40, 41, and 42. The first picture is of a typical balled-and-burlapped dwarf Mugo pine as it came from the nursery. Figure 40 is a photograph made an hour later, after pruning and potting. At this stage the container is much too deep to meet traditional standards, but it is a safer intermediate step, requiring less drastic root pruning at the start. Figure 41 shows the same plant repotted the next season. The sketch, Figure 42, suggests one possible style of training that could be carried out by pruning and wiring.

In starting with older plants, such as these, it is highly desirable to choose those with naturally interesting trunks and basically good branching, as these thicker members are not so easily changed. After that the qualities sought are those valued for all bonsai—the proportions that contribute grace and an impression of size. Not just any nursery plant, then, will serve for rapid conversion to bonsai, but part of the pleasure of collecting plants is this search for potential specimens.

In addition to older plants that have already developed qualities of character, there are younger plants more readily found in retail nurseries that may be enjoyed in a beginning collection. Still young and supple, they may be shaped to interesting forms in a short time. In the

Pruning and potting made this change in appearance of a dwarf Mugo pine.

Figure 39. The balled-and-burlapped nursery plant.

Figure 40. An hour later.

Figure 41. This 8-inch "tree" the next spring.

Main branch trained as apex

This branch brought down

Smaller pot to improve proportions

Remove altogether eventually

Articulate and bring down branch thus

Figure 42. Sketch suggesting plans for further development by pruning and wiring.   JAMES R. RAKER

smallest sizes are rooted cuttings and seedlings of diminutive proportions available from some nurseries, although most retail establishments do not sell them at this stage. In the wholesale trade they are known as "liners" because they are ready to be lined out in the field, or, nowadays, planted in containers for another year or two of growth to more valuable size. Some hobbyists have potted selections of these small plants as miniature bonsai, or used them in interesting group plantings.

SOME PLANTS SUITABLE FOR BONSAI AND ADAPTED BONSAI

Traditional bonsai trained by the Japanese are selections from ordinary trees, vines, and shrubs that normally grow to much greater size; most of them are species common to the temperate zone, requiring ordinary outdoor conditions for healthy growth; others are tender species that must be given special winter protection in colder climates. A few that are outstanding favorites with the Japanese—such as the short-leaf forms of Japanese white pine, Sargent juniper, and the Yeddo spruce—are difficult to find in this country. Most of the favored kinds, and many others, however, are readily available from nurseries here. As the characteristics sought in plants for bonsai (Chapter 9) are to be found in a great many species, a list of suitable plants could be very long.

At the end of this chapter are lists of some of the nursery-grown plants that have already proved good for training as bonsai or adapted bonsai. Many kinds are available from nurseries in almost all parts of the country, although probably not all listed here will be found at any one place. Nurseries tend to emphasize, of course, the species suitable to the local climate—spruces where it is cool and damp, for instance; certain junipers and pines, subtropicals and desert-adapted plants in the hot, dry areas. Many of the plants that are tender to cold in the North, however, may be found in the greenhouses of northern specialists in house and conservatory plants. A favorite kind of plant grown as bonsai in Hawaii, as an example, may be found also grown under glass in New Jersey.

Botanical names are of considerable importance in locating nursery plants, and the beginner in this kind of search should not consider them unduly formidable. They represent the only certain method of identifying plants, and nurserymen are familiar with them. Of course, some common names are entirely adequate; "pine" or "maple" will almost surely lead to plants of the right genus. But say "cypress" and you will find it applied to plants that are neither related nor particularly similar in appearance. Common names are of little help with plants that are uncommon, and are often misleading, even with well-known kinds. There are at least a dozen plants with shades of gray foliage called "dusty miller" in various parts of this country. Even a partial botanical name can mislead: the term "japonica" (which means simply "Japanese" and is part of the botanical name of many species) in parts of the South is used to designate *Camellia japonica*; a hundred miles or so north, it is applied to flowering quince, *Chaenomeles japonica*.

The lists that follow—subject to the limitations and modifications suggested above—are of plants to be found in nurseries. In general, they are not to be found growing wild, although infrequently some varieties may naturalize. Native wild species, some of which are also grown by nurseries, will be found named in the next chapter.

There is not complete agreement on the pronunciation of botani-cal names, but the phonetical versions here should be recognizable. The following list is of hardy plants sold by nurseries in most parts of the country:

Acer (ay′ ser) – maple, especially Japanese maple (*A. palmatum*) and its varieties, and trident maple (*A. buergerianum*)

Azalea (az zay′ lee uh) – esp. Satsuki and Kurume varieties

Berberis (ber′ ber iss) – barberry, esp. warty barberry (*B. verruculosa*) and Japanese barberry (*B. thunbergi*) var. Crimson Pygmy

Buxus (bux′ us) – boxwood, especially small-leaf forms of *B. microphylla*

Cedrus (seed′ rus) *atlantica* and *deodara* – atlas cedar and deodar cedar (true old-world cedars)

Chaenomeles (kee nom′ el eez) – flowering quince, several kinds

Chamaecyparis (kam ee sip′ ar iss) – false cypress, especially forms of Hinoki (*C. obtusa*) and Sawara cypress (*C. pisifera*)

Crataegus (krat teeg′ us) – hawthorns, several species

Cotoneaster (kot toh nee ass′ ter) – dwarf forms, several species

Cryptomeria (krip to meer′ ee uh) *Japonica* – cryptomeria

Fagus (fay′ gus) *sylvatica* – European beech

Ginkgo (gink′ go) – ginkgo

Ilex (eye′ lex) – holly, several species and varieties, esp. dwarf and small-leaf forms

Jasminum (jass′ min um) – jasmine

Juniperus (joo nip′ er us) – juniper, several species, many varieties

Larix (lar′ ix) – larch

Ligustrum (lig gust′ rum) – privet, ligustrum, several varieties

Malus (may′ lus) – crab apple, many varieties

Metasequoia (met a see quoy′ a) – dawn redwood

Picea (pye′ see uh) – spruce, several species and varieties, esp. Norway spruce (*P. Abies*, varieties *conica, gregoryana*, etc.)
Colorado spruce (*P. pungens*)
others

Pinus (pye' nus) – pine, esp. Japanese black pine (*P. thunbergii*), Scotch pine (*P. sylvestris*), and Mugo pine (*P. Mugo*)

Pseudolarix (soo doh lar' ix) *amabilis* – golden larch

Pyracantha (pye ruh kanth' uh) *coccinea* – fire thorn

Taxus (tax' us) – yew, several varieties

Zelkova (zel koh' va) *serrata* – zelkova

Less hardy species and varieties favored in the SOUTH, SOUTHWEST, and WEST COAST:

Bambusa (bam bew' suh) *multiplex* – var. Chinese Goddess and other varieties of bamboo

Camellia sasanqua and *hiemalis* – Camellia, esp. *C. hiemalis* varieties Shishi-Gashira and Bonsai Baby

Carissa (kar riss' uh) – Carissa, several kinds

Citrus – kumquat, calomondin, others

Cycas (sye' kass) *revoluta* – sago palm, cycad

Cyperus (sye peer' us) *alternifolius gracilis* – slender umbrella plant

Feijoa (fay joh' uh) *calleianum* – pineapple guava

Juniperus (joo nip' er us) – many species and varieties of juniper, including *J. chinensis torulosa*

Lagerstroemia (lay gur streem' ee uh) *indica* – crape myrtle

Olea (oh' lee uh) *europaea* – olive

Prunus (proon' us) *mume* – Japanese apricot, many varieties

Punica (pew' nik uh) – pomegranate, esp. dwarf forms

Pittosporum (pit tosp' or um, or pit is por' um) – pittosporum

Psidium (sid' ee um) *cattleianum* – strawberry guava

Pyracantha (pye ruh kanth' uh) – fire thorn, more colorful varieties

Tamarix (tam' uh rix) – tamarisk, several kinds

Plants favored for bonsai or adapted bonsai in *Hawaii:*

Brassaia (bra sye' uh) *actinophylla* – Brassaia

Bougainvillea (boog in vill' ee uh) *glabra* – bougainvillea

Casuarina (kass yew uh rye' nuh) *equisetifolia* – ironwood or Australian pine

Cupressus (kew press' us) *funebris* – mourning cypress

Cycas (sye' kass) *revoluta* – sago palm

Delonix (dee lon' icks) *regia* – royal poinciana

Eugenia (yew jeen' ee uh) *uniflora* – Eugenia

Ficus (fye' kus) *retusa* – Chinese banyan

Ixora (ik soh' ruh) *coccinea* – Chinese ixora

Juniperus (joo nip' er us), esp. *J. barbadensis* – Bermuda juniper, and *J. sargentii*

Pinus (pye' nus) *thunbergii* – Japanese black pine

Psidium (sid' ee um) *cattleianum* – strawberry guava

Chapter 5

Collect Specimens from "Your Own Backyard"

Of all the ways to acquire plants for bonsai the one with the most appeal for many of us is to dig them from the wild. This sounds like a pleasant outdoor pursuit with the allurement of a fishing trip, the prize in this case a plant that costs nothing, but may have priceless qualities. In truth, some old bonsai do have this background, their character developed by natural forces, the measurement of their age based on an estimate (often generous) of the years they grew wild before conversion added to the time they have been trained and potted for display.

Unfortunately, digging up naturally dwarfed plants is a most hazardous procedure, demanding the greatest care, and often destined to end in failure. The experience of the typical weekend outing, when wild flowers are brought home for our gardens, is bad enough; attempts to move old trees that have been dwarfed by adverse conditions are likely to be much worse. Digging a good root system is the main difficulty. The underground spread sometimes is amazing, as I found, in one case, where no feeder roots were uncovered closer than fifty-nine inches from the trunk of a pine that was only thirty-one inches tall. In addition to the likelihood of poor rootage, older plants in general lack the vigor of youth, so are slow to recover.

What is specifically suggested by "collecting" in this chapter is the way to handle plants which were not originally grown for bonsai, on the home grounds, or in the wild where digging them is permitted. Good conservation practices, of protecting our native plants, are implicit in the intent of those who have an understanding of the art of bonsai. Furthermore, there are laws to curb those people who are not innate conservationists.

There is danger both to our heritage of native plant life, and to the would-be bonsai grower himself, if "collecting" is undertaken indiscriminately. Plants should be collected from your own property,

Many native plants in the United States are adaptable to bonsai culture, but collecting naturally dwarfed specimens usually requires skill and patience. The foot-tall pine (Pinus virginiana), Figure 43, one of the short-leaf kinds in the East, would be passed up as "impossible" in its position growing in a 30-ton boulder. The gnarled specimen of sparkleberry (Vaccinium arboreum) on a south Georgia hillside, Figure 44, will require patient step-by-step root pruning before it may be safely moved.

Figure 43

Figure 44. Gnarled specimen of sparkleberry.

or where permission has been obtained from the owner—not from the roadside, nor from places where outings are enjoyed in the country. Remember, where fishing and other recreational activities are permitted, on public or private lands, this permission does not extend to the right to remove plants. In State and National Parks the disturbance of native plants is expressly forbidden, and violations are severely dealt with. Private-property owners rightly consider removal of plants as theft.

Fortunately, there are opportunities for hobbyists to collect plants in a legitimate manner. I know of cases where bonsai clubs have gained permission from forestry authorities to dig certain kinds of plants in specific areas where their removal would not be a loss. And an even more widespread opportunity is to be found in the plants in "our own backyard." The Japanese frequently convert old plants from orchard or garden. Part of the pleasure in the hobby of bonsai is in visualizing plants in this new role, and an old shrub or volunteer seedling in your own garden may be a prime choice. Such plants at home or nearby offer another advantage: it will be convenient to give

Two native species of the West skillfully collected and trained by JOHN NAKA, *of Los Angeles.*

Figure 45a. Golden cup oak (Quercus chrysolepis) 26 inches.

Figure 45b. California juniper (Juniperus californica) 40 inches.

them occasional attention in training the upper parts simultaneously with the development of a new compact root system. The angle of trunk may be altered somewhat, and branches brought into place to fill the composition, either by spiral wiring or tying with soft string. Drastic pruning may be in order, and this is especially desirable if the old roots are similarly cut back a great deal.

For older plants good results are most assured when the operation is carried out carefully, at the most favorable time of the year, with consistent follow-up attention. Several modern aids to plant culture may be used to increase the chances for success and to make the process less time consuming.

Plants growing in one's garden are often good candidates for ·bonsai. This Ibota privet (Ligustrum obtusifolium) represents a kind of bonsai that might have spent some years growing in a garden as a large plant. Drastic root and top pruning, followed by training of a new shallow root system and compact branch and twig structure, can develop such a plant into an impressive specimen.

Figure 46

STEP BY STEP A SAFER WAY

For those who will take the time, by far the safer way to move an old plant, under most circumstances, is to follow a step-by-step procedure of root pruning. This may require two or three years. Usually, the initial work is to dig a trench one third or halfway around the plant, within six inches or a foot of the base, cutting major roots that extend beyond this space, then backfilling the trench with good dirt that will encourage development of new compact rootage. The most favorable time for this operation is during the dormant season, although it is often safe to do a little root pruning at other times of the year as well. The following year the root pruning is carried farther.

In successful collecting of wild plants, a later step in the procedure is as important as the transfer itself: having a place ready for the plant. This may be a large pot or wooden box containing a sandy-soil mixture, or a well-drained ground bed in part sun that can be shaded at first and is convenient for watering. Replanting immediately is most important.

TOOLS

Equipment for collecting wild plants may be simple and compact enough to go into the pocket of a hunting jacket. Basic needs are something for pruning and digging, and materials to keep the roots moist until replanted. Garden pruners, a trowel, and a piece of wet burlap wrapped in a sheet of plastic and tied with a string will do.

For more ambitious work a pruning or keyhole saw is useful. A camper's spade or an army-surplus entrenching tool will facilitate digging, especially if the digging edge is first sharpened with a file to make severing roots easy. The sizes of burlap and plastic sheets will be determined by the size of the plants sought, but it is well to have them ample. Plastic bags are convenient for smaller plants, moss, and the like. Plastic ones sold as garbage-pail liners or the polyethylene type used for freezing foods do nicely.

TIME

By far the best season for collecting plants is in late winter and early spring, just before and as growth starts, as indicated by swelling buds. A second fairly favorable time for some species is in early fall, when plants are comparatively dormant but the roots still active enough to become re-established before winter. The season to avoid, if possible, is when the plant has just come into full new leaf in spring.

Out-of-season transplanting can be successful, although even greater than usual care will probably still result in a lower batting average. Midsummer is not as unfavorable as is commonly thought, for then many plants have checked their growth, new wood is maturing, and there is ample time for new roots to form before winter. At this period removing half or more of the leaves of deciduous plants is helpful. With needled species unnecessary branches and twigs should be pruned, but the plants should not be defoliated. Shading and frequent daily syringing are vital to plants collected in summer. Mid-winter collecting in milder climates may be done also, but the plants thereafter should not be exposed to extreme cold or drying winds. Keep them in a light protected place, where the temperature stays somewhat above freezing until spring.

METHOD

For collecting a potentially valuable plant, here are the steps that might be followed: Study the plant for form, then prune all twigs and branches that you are sure will not be needed in the ultimate development. Sometimes a five- or six-foot plant may be reduced to one or two feet at this time. A modern aid can be used at this stage to lessen the hazard to the plant. Drench the plant, both leaves and trunk, with an antidesiccant spray of the kind used by nurserymen to facilitate transplanting difficult nursery stock. This material forms a transparent coating of plastic or latex that prevents excessive moisture loss while, at the same time, permits air and light to pass through. It is available in several brands, and small plastic spray bottles of it are on the market for home gardeners. Do not rely on this measure to take the place of other precautions, however.

If possible, start digging two or three feet from the trunk, working inward, and combing the soil from the roots with an outward motion, and at the same time carefully preserving these roots. Nearer the trunk leave a ball of undisturbed soil, from eight inches to a foot or two in diameter, according to the size of the plant. Cut the taproot, but preserve as much of it as you can, especially with pines. If the digging process takes much time, be sure to keep exposed roots covered with wet burlap or damp soil. Finally, wrap the roots and earth ball with the burlap and tie up in the sheet of plastic.

It is usually a good idea to bring home some of the soil where the plant grew originally for incorporation in the mixture used in its new location. Soil at the plant's original location, however, is not necessarily suitable for use in a container. If one of the environmental factors that caused natural dwarfing was a tight clay soil of poor quality, exclusive use of it in a container can prove fatal. A well-drained potting mixture, described in Chapter 11, is satisfactory for almost all kinds of plants.

On the way home protect the plant from wind, sun, and heat, and if the trip is a long one, syringe the foliage occasionally with water to prevent wilting. Replant promptly and put the plant in a light place shaded from direct sun and screened from the wind. Spraying the foliage with water several times a day, especially in sunny weather, is very helpful in encouraging new growth. If this is not practical, wrapping the trunk and larger limbs with strips of cloth will aid in keeping the plant from drying out. The soil should be kept moist at the roots, but not sodden. After about a month there should be evidence of some recovery, at which time sunlight may be permitted and less frequent waterings applied.

An alternate to this way of shading and watering would be to use the mist-propagation method and more sunlight during the first of the postoperative period. This technique is described in the next chapter under "Cuttings."

Training of collected plants, other than pruning, should not be started until they show healthy recovery.

Lists at the end of this chapter are of a few native species in this country that have already proved adaptable to a bonsai style of training. The geographical divisions suggested here are not exact. Species overlap certain areas, are nonexistent in many places within their normal zone. Some natives are confined to small sections in the Smoky Mountains, as an example, while others are to be found widely, from Canada to Florida and far into the Midwest.

Botanical names are of less help in locating wild native plants, although they still are the final means of accurate identification. Nurserymen know the plants they grow but are not necessarily familiar with native species that are not grown commercially. As usual common names can be misleading, and sometimes they are known only in a limited area. In my part of the southeastern United States, the Eastern or Canadian hemlock (*Tsuga canadensis*) is commonly called "spruce pine," a fair reflection of a confused botanical background of this species which was shifted by taxonomists from pine, spruce, and fir to its present genus.

Most of the following list of plants suitable for bonsai or adapted bonsai are available from general nurseries or those that specialize in native species:

EASTERN UNITED STATES

Balsam fir – *Abies balsamea* (Northeast)
Beech – *Fagus grandifolia*
Birch – *Betula papyrifera* and *populiafolia*, white and gray birch
White cedar – *Chamaecyparis thyoides*
Red cedar – *Juniperus virginiana*
Cypress – *Taxodium distichum* and *ascendens*, bald and pond cypress (South)
Hawthorn – *Crataegus*, several species
Hemlock – *Tsuga canadensis* and *caroliniana*
Holly – *Ilex*, several species; esp. Possum haw—*I. decidua*; Yaupon—*I. vomitoria* (South) and black alder—*I. verticillata*
Hornbeam – *Carpinus caroliniana*
Ironwood – *Ostrya virginiana*
Juniper – *Juniperus*, esp. dwarf and prostrate varieties of common juniper— *J. communis*
Larch or tamarack – *Larix laricina*
Pine – *Pinus*, several species, esp. short-leaf forms of Jack, pitch, scrub and mountain pine—*P. echinata, rigida, Banksiana* and *virginiana*
Redbud – *Cercis canadensis*
Sand myrtle – *Leiophyllum*, esp. dwarf *L. Lyoni*
Sparkleberry or farkleberry – *Vaccinium arboreum*
Sour Gum or pepperidge, or black gum or tupelo – *Nyssa aquatica* and *sylvatica*
Spruce – *Picea*, several species (North)
Sweet Gum – *Liquidambar styraciflua*

WESTERN UNITED STATES

Ceanothus or California wild lilac – *Ceanothus*, several species and vars.
Arizona cypress – *Cupressus arizonica*
Lawson cypress or Port Orford cedar – *Chamaecyparis Lawsoniana*
Nootka, Sitka, or Yellow cypress – *Chamaecyparis nootkatensis*
Desert Willow – *Chilopsis linearis* (Southwest)
Douglas fir – *Pseudotsuga*
Hawthorn – *Crataegus*, several species
Western Hemlock – *Tsuga heterophylla* (Northwest)
Incense cedar or white cedar – *Libocedrus decurrens*
Juniper – *Juniperus*, several species, many varieties
Manzanita – *Arctostaphylos Manzanita*, and other Western species
Mesquite – *Prosopis* (Southwest)

Golden cup oak – *Quercus chrysolepis*
California live oak – *Quercus agrifolia*
California scrub oak – *Quercus dumosa*
Pine – *Pinus*, several species, esp. Pinion pine and its various forms—*P. cembroides* or *edulis*; Shore pine—*P. contorta*, and Bishop pine—*P. muricata*
Redbud – *Cercis occidentalis*, Western redbud
Big sagebrush – *Artemisia tridentata* (Southwest)
Spruce – *Picea*, several species (Northwest)

HAWAII

(native or naturalized species)
Lehua – *Metrosideros collina*
Ohia – *Eugenia malaccensis*
Ohelo – *Vaccinium reticulatum*
Pukiawe – *Styphelia tameiameiae*
Ti – *Cordyline terminalis*

Chapter 6

Other Ways to Start Plants at Home—Importing Bonsai

For those who are interested in starting plants at home for later development as bonsai, the usual methods of plant propagation are described here. In addition, at the end of this chapter some of the problems of importing bonsai from Japan are discussed.

SEEDS

Sowing seeds is an inexpensive way to acquire certain species, some of them not readily available as plants. A few kinds grow rather quickly to become decorative when planted in small forestlike groves, or as small potted specimens, although the general rule is that it takes several years for seedlings to acquire much of the stature of bonsai.

Germinating the seed of long-lived plants of the less well-known kinds can be a challenge to experts as well as to home gardeners whose experience often has been limited to popular annual flowers and vegetables. Annual plants must reproduce each year, so most kinds have vigorously sprouting seed. Some perennials, and especially shrubs and trees that survive as individuals for many years, are usually more demanding of the exact conditions for their seeds to start growth. This may involve a built-in timing device in the seeds that is calculated to delay germination until a favorable season for the particular species in its usual climate zone.

About the only safe broad generalization is that in the case of many tropicals, subtropicals and some hardy species whose seeds mature early in the year, the seeds will sprout quickly if fresh ones are sown. Seeds of citrus sometimes start to grow before the fruit is cut, and seeds of some maples will come up within two weeks. On the other hand, seeds of many species native to temperate zones respond only to specialized treatment. Some holly seeds regularly lie dormant for two years. Nurserymen have worked out practical methods in improving the germination rate of known varieties: seeds of stone fruits (plum, apricot, etc.) may be kept moist until planted; pulpy seeds, such as dogwood, are depulped mechanically or by soaking a few days; seeds with hard or waxy coats sometimes are nicked with a file or treated with acid.

Many seeds lie dormant through a winter season and require this period of cold to trigger them to active life. These are often treated by a method known as stratification, so called because originally the seed and damp sand were assembled in layers. Today the seed usually is just mixed with damp sand, exposed to winter cold in a container protected by screen wire or in some other manner against such enemies as mice. In spring the seeds are sown in the field or special beds.

A convenient method of stratification at home is to put the seed-damp sand mixture in a plastic bag and store it about two months in a refrigerator. If in doubt about the need for this cold treatment, divide the quantity of seed in half, sow one part directly, stratify the other and sow them later.

For starting seeds a variety of containers are practical, including cans with drainage holes punched in them, or shallow pots known as bulb pans. In place of soil, a mixture of peat moss and sand, half and half mixed thoroughly, can be used, or a sandy soil, or any not-rich, well-drained potting-soil mixture. Disease is a serious danger to many seedlings, so if soil or leafmold is employed, it is prudent to sterilize it first. One way to do this is to put a shallow pan of the material in the oven at 200 degrees for about an hour. Fill the containers with whatever soil mixture is used, press seeds into place, spaced apart on the surface, and cover lightly. Water by standing the container in a pan of water, or with a gentle spray.

One way to greatly minimize the attention required and, at the same time, maintain the necessary even degree of moisture, is to put the seed pots in polyethylene plastic bags, of the kind used for storing foods in freezers. First be sure the container has drained thoroughly. Then place it in the bag and it will need no further attention except a frequent check to see when germination has begun. As soon as seedlings start to appear, the container must be removed from the bag, placed where it will get some sunlight, and watered regularly. When the second or third set of leaves appears, transplant the seedlings to individual pots. Or, seedlings can be left in place until the following year. If in a peat-and-sand mixture, the seedlings should be fed with a weak solution of liquid fertilizer.

Varieties that require stratification are best sown in early spring, although seeds treated this way in a refrigerator usually can be induced to grow at any season. If there is a cool place with ample light available, many seedlings may be kept growing, to some extent, through the first winter. All kinds should be given some protection, even the hardiest ones, this first winter, in a cool greenhouse or a protected frame. Tender tropicals, of course, must always be protected from frost.

Here are some varieties that may be started from seed, with suggested treatment:

Fresh seeds to be sown immediately: HARDY SPECIES—Maple, elm, oak, buckeye (*Aesculus* species) and chestnut. (These will germinate the next spring also.)

TROPICALS AND SUBTROPICALS—Citrus, chinaberry (*Melia azedarach*), Chinese parasol tree (*Firmiana simplex*), *Jacaranda acutifolia, Leucaena glauca, Calliandra surinaemensis,* and silk oak (*Grevellia robusta*).

Seeds to be stratified: Apple, beech, crab apple, barberry, flowering cherry, quince, peach, holly, cotoneaster, pyracanthas, hawthorn, ginkgo, dogwood, linden, juniper, and yew.

Seeds that can be kept dry until spring: Cryptomeria, pine, larch, hemlock, spruce, sophora.

Seeds that germinate more evenly if depulped: Barberry, cotoneaster, dogwood, and holly.

The following three methods of plant propagation—by cuttings, layering, and grafting—are time-honored garden practices for reproducing plants with the same characteristics as their parents. Each has its advantages and limitations for the bonsai collector:

CUTTINGS

Relatively short cuttings of twigs or branches of many plants may be induced to grow roots if kept under the right conditions of light and moisture, the results being strongly influenced by the ability of the species to so react, and the time of year when the cuttings are made, as well as the care given them. Modern techniques have so reduced the required attention that the home gardener, with little more than household items, can use this method to advantage, even though bonsai specimens are not quickly achieved. Cuttings often are easily come by, and even trimmings of your own bonsai or shrubs can be used.

The season when the cuttings are made is a vital factor with most kinds of plants. Professional propagators find that the difference of thirty days can alter results drastically, in some cases. However, for the hobbyists working with small numbers of plants at home, this is one case where I would say, when in doubt go ahead and try. The expenditure of time and effort is not great, and often cuttings root readily, although in theory the season is not quite right.

In general, soft-wood cuttings, made of new growth in spring or early summer, root most rapidly, but are often difficult to keep from wilting to the point of no return. Chrysanthemums are an example of a common garden plant regularly started from such tender new growth.

The longer list of woody plants root more easily from half-ripened or semihardwood cuttings made in early summer, when new growth has matured but not yet become brittle. Varieties include azalea, barberry, daphne, some conifers, cotoneaster, fire thorn (*Pyracantha*), jasmine, pieris, and false cypress (*Chamaecyparis*).

New plants of many species may be started from cuttings. The usual practice is to cut twigs or branches into lengths from 2 to 6 inches long, and then remove the lower leaves, Figure 47. Dipping the ends in a hormonelike rooting stimulant encourages stronger root development, Figure 48. A homemade propagating case is shown in Figure 49, devised from a grape box filled with peat moss and sand (as the rooting medium), and covered with a sheet of plastic held up on ribs made from coat hangers.

Figure 47

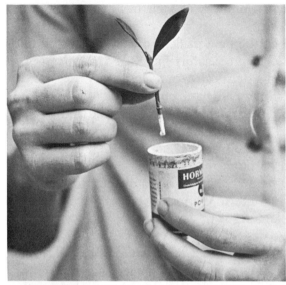

Figure 48

Figure 49

Traditionally, some kinds are easily started from hardwood cuttings made in autumn, of such plants as arborvitae, crape myrtle, pomegranate, quince, willow, and wisteria.

TOOLS

All that is absolutely required are a sharp knife or pruners, and a rooting medium that may be kept shaded and watered. Sandy soil can be used, but several special rooting mixtures have considerable advantage in encouraging better root growth and in preventing disease. A good material is an expanded rock product called perlite; another one is vermiculite. A standard mixture long used is sand mixed with undecayed peat moss.

Two modern materials may greatly speed and simplify the operation: One is a rooting stimulant, for sale in garden stores. This is available in a small packet, or in a three-grade combination suitable for a wide range of plants. The other is polyethylene plastic of the kind used for such household items as freezer bags and covered refrigerator dishes.

METHOD

Cuttings preferably are two to six inches long, cut one-fourth to one-half inch below a leaf, or it may be a slip that has been pulled from a larger branch. If the cuttings are not immediately planted, they should be kept moist by wrapping in wet cloth. With a suitable rooting medium at hand, in a container or frame: first, trim cuttings to the desired length and remove the lower leaves; second, dip the lower cut end into the hormone powder; and third, insert the lower half or more of the cutting into the rooting medium.

A convenient combination for propagating cuttings is a six-inch pot, filled with the rooting mixture, and a plastic polyethylene freezer bag. Fill the pot with the mixture, water it evenly and allow it to drain thoroughly. After inserting the cuttings, set the pot inside a plastic bag large enough to give some air space above the cuttings, and fasten the top together with a clip or rubber band. A plastic refrigerator dish can serve in a similar capacity. In this case, because there are no drainage holes, it is imperative to drain the rooting medium very thoroughly, as it is as disastrous for cuttings to be kept too wet as it is too dry. I have found such a container particularly handy for very short cuttings of dwarf-plant varieties.

One material that is particularly well adapted for use in a closed container is sphagnum moss, which appears to have an almost anti-biotic resistance to damping off disease which destroys so many young plants. This is the moss frequently used by nurserymen to pack around the roots of plants to be shipped. As a rooting medium, it may be bought already milled, or it can be prepared by rubbing it through a half-inch wire screen. The dry moss is then soaked in water, handfuls squeezed to remove excessive moisture, and then packed lightly into the bottom of the container. Cuttings are inserted in the usual way.

With such closed plastic containers, no further watering is needed, even though months may elapse. The containers should be placed where they get good light but not direct sunlight.

MIST PROPAGATION

A relatively new method that has greatly speeded the rooting of some kinds of cuttings and made possible the growing of others previously thought impossible to start from cuttings, is known as mist propagation. In this method, either continuous or intermittent mist is used to keep the foliage wet, thus preventing wilting and permitting soft-wood cuttings to be placed in strong light, even full sun. Sunlight encourages growth, but normally too much of it causes wilting, which, carried too far, results in death of the cutting. Prior to this new procedure, propagators had to tread the fine line of shading enough to prevent wilting, but allowing as much light as possible to encourage root growth.

Perfect drainage, shelter from wind, and a porous rooting medium, such as sand or perlite, are the essentials. Cuttings can be kept under continuous mist created by special, very fine spray nozzles three feet or so above the beds, or better results come sometimes from intermittent mist. This may be adjusted by a clock-timing device. Or, at least two kinds of switches have been devised that start the spray as the leaves begin to dry, then stop it when they are thoroughly wet. One is based on an electric current affected by moisture; the other is a bit of screen wire that collects droplets until it becomes heavy enough to close the valve, and opens it again as it dries and becomes lighter.

Bonsai growers might find this mist method helpful in re-establishing collected old plants, as well as for the rooting of the more difficult older cuttings.

AFTERCARE

By whatever means roots are induced to develop, all cuttings pass through a critical period of adjustment to the normal life of a plant. After roots are well established, the plants should go through a hardening period when they get less constant moisture, are exposed to more light and air movement. In the case of mist-propagated plants, it is good practice to feed several times with a weak, soluble fertilizer, applied to both foliage and soil, to counteract the loss of nutrients from the washing action of the mist. With plants started by home methods suggested above, the transition can be started by opening the sheltering enclosure for a few hours each day for a week, then slowly increasing the exposure to full air and light. In this case, also, it is helpful to water with a half-strength liquid fertilizer a few days before transplanting.

Rooted cuttings may be individually potted, or moved to frames or shaded beds for several months or until the next year. In transplanting, care should be taken not to break off the new roots, whose attachment to the stem, at first, is quite brittle.

CUTTINGS RELATIVELY EASY TO ROOT:

Willow, boxwood, English and Boston ivies, euonymus, fire thorn, azalea, barberry, tamarisk, privet, juniper, arborvitae, yew, metasequoia, cryptomeria, Japanese holly, pieris, and crape myrtle.

PLANTS CONSIDERED DIFFICULT, or sometimes impossible to start from cuttings, although some are now handled successfully under mist: Fir, hemlock, pine, locust, mimosa, redbud, ginkgo, mountain laurel, golden raintree, blue spruce, wax myrtle, and most fruit trees.

LAYERING

Layering is a way to get roots to form on a branch or trunk while it is still part of the parent plant. Normally, it is used in propagating certain species that are difficult or impossible to start from cuttings, or to start plants from older wood. This latter possibility is of interest to bonsai growers, but unfortunately the older the wood, the slower and more uncertain the response to such treatment.

Injuring the bark tissue of the plant, and then keeping this area enclosed in a damp rooting medium until roots form, are the basic steps in layering. There are three general ways to carry out this process. In the first one, especially with some of the multistem shrubs and the kinds of trees that sucker readily, or send out new stems from the roots, the soil is merely mounded around the base of the plant. Some species, when so treated, will form new rooted suckers, even without wounding the stem tissue.

In the second method, a branch long and low enough to easily reach the ground is buried at one point, with the end of the branch protruding. A slanting cut about two inches long is made in the upper (or lower) side of the branch, and this is held open by partially twisting the end of the branch or by wedging it with a sliver of wood or a small pebble.

The third method, called air layering, is a great leap forward over the ancient version known as "Chinese layering," in which soil or moss around a branch was kept moist by patient Oriental gardeners who watered them several times a day over long periods of time. Today, plastics and hormonelike root stimulants eliminate much of the time and attention required, but not all of the uncertainty.

In air layering, the wound on the branch, made six to eighteen inches from the end of the branch, may be by a shallow slanting cut, or by peeling a half-inch strip of bark all around the stem. Dust the cut with hormone powder. Cut off leaves within six inches of the

Air layering, illustrated here with a large-leaf plant not suitable for bonsai, may require a few weeks or a year or more for roots to develop.

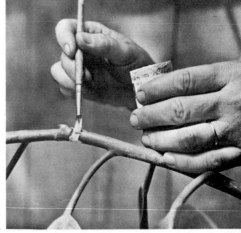

Figure 50. Remove strip of bark.

Figure 51. Dust with rooting stimulant.

wound. Now soak sphagnum moss (not sieved or milled) in water, take a handful and squeeze it tightly to remove excess moisture, then form a fist-size ball of the damp moss around the branch to cover the wounded area. Wrap the ball tightly with a sheet of polyethylene plastic, with a folded overlap. Finally, twist the ends of the plastic around the branch top and bottom and fasten securely with plastic electrical tape.

Branches layered in spring frequently root by the next spring, but

Figure 52. Enclose in damp sphagnum moss.

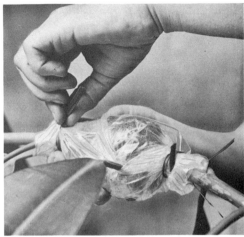

Figure 53. Fold and tie plastic around the moss.

Figure 54. Roots may become visible in time.

Figure 55. New roots basis for new plant.

those treated in fall may require until the second spring. In many cases, no further watering is needed. If the time required is prolonged, it may be necessary to reopen the top of the ball, and water. Be sure the top is sealed sufficiently well with tape to prevent rain water from running into the moss, thus causing a supersaturated condition that would prevent rooting. Roots usually are visible through the plastic, when they have formed, at which time the layer may be cut from the parent plant and treated like a rooted cutting.

The better times for layering are early spring and late summer. With all three methods root stimulants may prove helpful in developing vigorous roots, in the same way they are with cuttings.

GRAFTING

Grafting is widely used by commercial growers of fruit trees and certain ornamentals of varieties that would not come true from seed. The technique is based on the fact that if the cambium layer—the living tissue that lies between the outer bark and the inner wood—of two compatible plants are put in contact with each other at the right season, they tend to grow together. From the desired variety, cuttings (or sometimes leaf buds), called the scions, are made which are then grafted to another plant, called the understock. The top of the understock is immediately or ultimately removed, and the growth from the scion, furnished with the sap from the understock, is thereafter exactly like the parent plant that furnished the scion wood.

There is limited application of grafting to bonsai, largely because the point of union of scion and stock is unsightly in a small plant. Bud grafts result in an abruptly crooked stem, and most other methods show a difference in trunk size and/or color of bark. The Japanese do employ grafting, however, in order to reproduce valued characteristics found only in selected plants. For instance, short-needled forms of white pine are grafted on black-pine seedlings, or a type of pine with interesting corky bark furnishes the scion. Often scions of a named variety of flowering apricot are grafted on an old stump, thus quickly producing an ancient specimen. It is also possible, by grafting, to start a point of growth on a picturesque trunk that is otherwise lacking in good branch or root placement.

The critical point is timing. Normally, the procedure is to graft in late winter or very early spring, using dormant scions on stocks that have just begun to have a rising flow of sap. An easy way to have dormant scions at the proper time is to make the cuttings ahead of time, and then store them in tightly sealed plastic bags in a refrigerator. There are exceptions to this timing: Budding is done in early summer, employing a dormant bud at the base of a leaf inserted in the stock, while the bark is still growing, is loosely attached and will slip. Pines are grafted in spring by immediately transferring a tip cutting from the parent to the stock plant.

Equipment needed: A very sharp knife, strips of waxed cloth, or raffia, or (preferably) special rubber grafting bands and grafting wax. Special tools are sometimes used in budding and cleft grafting, but are not essential.

The cambium layers of scion and stock are brought into contact, in the case of cleft grafting, by cutting off the top of the stock and splitting this stump end; then cutting the bottom end of the scion into a long wedge that is inserted into the slit. If the scion is smaller than the stock, it is placed to one edge, so the bark on one side of both parts are in alignment. A screwdriver can conveniently hold open the slit end while this is done. If the stock does not hold the scion securely enough, it is bound up and, in any case, all the exposed area is covered with grafting wax to prevent drying. Unfortunately, the easier forms of grafting, such as cleft grafting and budding, leave the most objectionable scars. There are many other ways to graft, including useful veneer and bark grafts that are described in detail in several good books on the subject.

IMPORTING BONSAI FROM JAPAN

Since the Plant Quarantine Act of 1919 set up regulations to prevent the entry of hitchhiking pests and diseases on plants and fruits brought into this country by importers, immigrants, and tourists, the shipment of bonsai from Japan has been strictly limited. No plants may be imported with soil around the roots, a restriction particularly hazardous to most evergreens and older plants. All plants permitted entry must first be subject to fumigation or other treatment, another handicap to survival, although inspectors report that most losses, at this stage, are due to delays, plants arriving in poor condition, or shipment out of season.

Many species that are particularly popular with the Japanese, such as Yeddo spruce, maple, bamboo, and flowering apricot, are on a list totally barred, because they are known to be potential disease carriers.

Juniper, jasmine, pomegranate, and wisteria are among another group subject to postentry quarantine in this country on approved premises controlled by the importer.

But plants can be imported successfully, with persistence and luck. Here are steps suggested to minimize the delays and hazards:

First, well in advance, write for the latest regulations, permits, and mailing labels from the U. S. Department of Agriculture, Plant Quarantine Division, Permit Section, 209 River Street, Hoboken, New Jersey.

Second, time the shipment for the dormant season, between mid-December and the first of March. If you are traveling in Japan, find a nurseryman who can label the variety with the correct botanical name inside the package, and who will pack the bare roots with damp sphagnum moss.

The importer has the responsibility to see that the plants are sent to the right inspection station for clearance, usually San Francisco, Seattle, Honolulu, San Pedro, or Hoboken. Customs clearance can be taken care of by the importer (you) in person, or by a customs broker he employs. This latter delaying action is not required for mail importations valued at less than $250, according to recent regulations. Therefore, air-mail packages of less than this value are expedited. Your numbered mailing label, secured in advance from the Permit Section, will assure prompt shipment to your home.

Deciduous plants on the enterable list have a somewhat better survival rate than the evergreens. These include birch (*Betula*), hornbeam (*Carpinus*), flowering quince (*Chaenomeles*), hawthorn (*Crataegus*), beech (*Fagus*), ginkgo, tamarix, bald cypress (*Taxodium*), and zelkova.

Enterable evergreens include azalea (*Rhododendron*), boxwood (*Buxus*), Japanese cedar or false cypress (*Chamaecyparis*), cryptomeria, pyracantha, and hemlock (*Tsuga*). Limited experience within my knowledge indicates that the better bets among the evergreens are the azaleas, junipers (subject to postentry quarantine), and cryptomeria.

The would-be importer operating from home base may find an additional difficulty in locating a Japanese nurseryman willing to undertake the transaction. The production of most of these plants in Japan is an individual or family matter. Like small businessmen almost everywhere, few are interested in export orders that involve problems of language and complex government regulations. There are signs that these barriers are being lowered somewhat. The full text of the

U. S. Department of Agriculture regulations on bonsai importation has been printed in both Japanese and English in Japanese bonsai magazines. Some skilled nurserymen in this country are now importing a few plants from time to time.

Chapter 7

The Container as Frame

The container is secondary in importance only to the bonsai plant itself. An appropriate one will go a long way toward showing the good qualities of even a mediocre plant. On the other hand, the tall red-clay pot commonly used in this country, and its connotations, will destroy the effectiveness of an otherwise superb specimen. The relationship of container to plant in bonsai often is likened to that of frame to picture. The Japanese, however, place an even higher value on the quality of the pot and the harmonious setting it creates.

Keeping the requirements of these special kinds of potted plants in mind makes it less difficult to find suitable containers, or to adapt commonplace market items. One can even make them. Prime qualities sought are not only those that appear in harmony with the illusive quality of bonsai, but also provide a place favorable for a healthy plant.

The size and shape of the container is important in bonsai. Without other objects to determine scale, it is difficult to judge the size of this young rooted cutting in Figure 56. *The true proportions can be seen in* Figure 121.

Figure 56

The container must remain secondary to the plant in color, form, and decoration so as not to compete with it, and notably, there is a distinct secondary size relationship. Classic proportions often cited are, of the total height of plant and pot, 80 per cent plant, 20 per cent container. For broader types of plants the ratio may be 60 per cent plant, 40 per cent container. Sometimes the plant may range as high as 90 per cent above the pot.

Shallow, traylike containers create a horizontal ground line suggesting a bit of landscape and making them suitable for many bonsai. Cascade-type plants, however, that extend over the side and reach to the base or even farther, require deep pots to maintain proper balance of weight and form. These special types, of course, must be kept on stands so the cascading growth will not be damaged and will show to advantage.

Plants trained in a slanting style also frequently are displayed in deeper, round containers—pots not as deep as for the cascades, but, perhaps, half as deep as they are wide.

Finally, bright, colorful glazes—characteristically used for Chinese potted plants, and once popular with the Japanese—now are avoided by bonsai growers.

Japanese preferences may prove a useful guide. Surveys of typical Japanese exhibits of outstanding plants probably would show: two thirds to three fourths of the pots in dark shades—dull red, gray, brown, dark purple, or in rare instances, a dark green; one fourth to one third of the containers in lighter tones of blue, gray and off-white. About three fourths would be unglazed. A few pots would have decorations limited, in most cases, to embossed designs or simple monochromatic sketches or Chinese characters on unglazed surfaces. Occasionally, a bronze tray, with the patina of age, would be found. A few group plantings might be grown on flat stones.

In the matter of color, the Japanese tend to follow these lines: pines and other conifers, most evergreens, and plants with dark-green leaves, in containers of dark colors; deciduous plants with light-green leaves or silvery trunks, lighter-colored pots. Brighter hues and high glazes sometimes are selected to harmonize with or contrast to the peak display of plants which are colorful by reason of flowers, fruit, or foliage. Green also is a color usually reserved for such plants. Glazed pots, some of them decorated and in bright shades, are sometimes used for *mame* bonsai, although some growers feel that this lessens the true bonsai quality of these toylike miniatures.

The value the Japanese place on the container is indicated by the fact that a substantial per cent of distinguished bonsai specimens in a public exhibit will be displayed in ancient Chinese pots, for which the owner probably paid what to the average Japanese amounts to a small fortune. Department stores in Japan regularly offer these imported antiques at prices up to several hundred dollars. Although containers made in their homelands may be of excellent quality, bonsai fanciers especially appreciate these examples of fine old pottery and enjoy indulging in the extravagance of buying one if they have a worthy plant.

The first consideration for maintaining a healthy plant is to see that the container has drainage holes in the bottom. There is no use in growing most plants suitable for bonsai without ample drainage. The Japanese do not try, and there is no reason to believe others are more skillful. Most pots have two drainage holes, and if they are large ones, they have several. The only exceptions are trays used to hold water for aquatic plants, or trees trained on rocks that hold them high above the water line.

Some Japanese believe that unglazed, porous pots contribute to a healthier environment for their bonsai. This is a factor in a humid climate as in Japan, where a prolonged rainy season starts in early summer. Glazed pots are approved, generally, for *mame* bonsai, where the small soil mass is difficult to keep moist. Plants of a larger size

Japanese pots often have two or more holes to assure drainage, Figure 57. The extra holes also are helpful when it is necessary to tie securely a tall plant in a shallow container.

Figure 57

Drainage holes are made easily in plastic pots and saucers with a hot soldering iron. Figure 58

Figure 58

also are more easily kept supplied sufficiently with moisture in very hot, dry climates, if they are in nonporous or glazed containers, with the right potting soil.

SOURCES

Wholesale importers now are bringing into this country a wide range of bonsai pots that may be found on the retail counters of nursery specialists or dealers in Oriental goods. A canvass of suppliers suggests the following: the most widely available color is an unglazed dark chocolate brown, a color rarely out of place with any bonsai; the predominating color presently available in glazed ware is blue, bright, light or dark; an additional color is a mixed glaze, mainly blue, but shading through green to brown. In lesser numbers there may be found a fairly wide range, from bright greens and shiny porcelain whites in the less desirable types, to a very few handsome grays, browns, bisque, and antique finishes.

Among useful shapes most commonly available is a rectangular pot, with square or rounded corners, with or without a lip extending outward. In proportions, the width is approximately two thirds the length. Sizes range from miniatures three inches long to large ones up to twenty-four inches. Depths vary from less than one inch to about four inches. Oval containers come in comparable sizes. These pots especially are useful for individual trees or groves.

Deep pots for cascades are available in square, round, and hexagonal shapes, usually slightly wider than deep, some of them bearing decorated panels. Round and hexagonal pots may be moderately deep or shallow, and are adaptable to individual trees, the round ones, in particular, to slanting styles, the hexagon to close-clustered groups.

Pots are imported usually in sets of three sizes nested together. To assure drainage, all Japanese pots have feet, in some cases inconspicuous, in others adding a decorative touch.

At the time when nursery stock is first moved to bonsai containers, I have found several pot sizes particularly useful because they make possible a minimum of root disturbance. For nursery plants grown in gallon cans or 8-inch pots, the shift is made rather easily to rectangular or oval bonsai containers approximately 11 inches long, 7 wide and 3 deep, to round or hexagonal pots 7 to 9 inches in diameter 3½ inches deep, and to cascade pots 8 inches across and 7 deep. Small plants for sale in 2½- or 3-inch pots may be reset in Japanese pots 4 inches wide and 3 inches deep. These small plants, of course, may be used in group plantings in much larger shallow containers.

DOMESTIC CONTAINERS

There are a few potters producing wares for bonsai in this country, but so far they are the exceptions. The good designers tend to create pottery too impressively beautiful in itself to play second fiddle to a plant; the less ambitious pottery works rarely offer anything in a usable shape. There are many shallow containers made for flower arrangements that can be adapted by providing holes for drainage, however. And there are possibilities even at the dime store, in plastic bowls for instance, if taste and ingenuity are used.

Making a hole in the bottom of a dish sounds like a dangerous operation, but actually it is rather easily accomplished with low-fired pottery types. Some of the high-fired glazed wares, which approach the brittleness of porcelain and glass, are indeed hazardous to handle, except with special tools. The wise course for expensive ware of this kind would be to take it to a glazier, who has special bits and carborundum dust that he can use on a drill press to cut holes of various sizes in glass.

Holes can be made at home in the bottom of earthenware pieces with an electric drill equipped with a carborundum bit of the kind sold at hardware stores for drilling in concrete. An easier way, I have found, is to use a center punch, or preferably a sharp ice pick, and a light hammer. To employ these simple tools, first place the container firmly on a bed of sand, so pressure is evenly distributed over the whole bottom, not just on one part or the legs. Place the point of the pick where the hole is desired, tap gently with the hammer, moving the point slightly from side to side as a tiny chipped spot is created. (Even with a drill such a starting point is desirable, the usual purpose of a center punch to mark the point for the drill.) If the chipped spot is slightly enlarged and light blows are continued at this point, with patience, the point will penetrate the pottery. Normally, a larger area breaks out on the underside. The initial small hole is enlarged by tapping out sections with the sharp point of the ice pick around the edges.

For plastic ware, drainage holes are made by using a hot soldering iron or wood-burning tool. I have seen an attractive container created from a shallow bowl, after drainage holes were made, by attaching small wooden feet with a waterproof glue and spraying the whole thing with a matte-finish lacquer or enamel.

Wood and cement, in the hands of a home craftsman, can be used to make suitable containers, especially as substitutes for the larger tray-pots which are quite expensive. Rot-resistant lumber, such as cypress and redwood, will last a number of years. If redwood is used, first drill for fasteners, to prevent splitting, and use aluminum or galvanized nails or screws, because a substance in redwood quickly destroys ordinary metal. If regular lumber is employed, treat it with a preservative, such as copper naphthenate available from paint dealers, but not with creosote which is toxic to plants.

Large containers may be made from concrete, and mixes in sacks, available at hardware stores, are suitable for this purpose. Such containers must be reinforced and to do this use a coarse wire screen laid midway between two layers of the wet mixture forming the bottom of the pot if the container is to be a shallow one. For deeper ones, use wire in both bottom and sides. A container of lighter weight results if you make your own mixture by employing perlite in place of the gravel and part of the sand, mixed with cement. Follow directions on the perlite bag.

TRAINING POTS

Inexpensive pots are a convenience in the early stages of training bonsai plants and are useful even in small collections. The standard clay pot, as tall as it is wide, with a tapering form, can be used for cascades, but shallower ones are needed for other plants. In the clay-pot line, there are shorter versions variously known as azalea and fern pots. The shallowest type widely available is called a bulb pan, because it is used by florists in forcing blubs for early bloom. Similar shapes also are to be found among plastic pots.

Useful shallow containers can be devised from plant saucers by making drainage holes in them. The clay ones are not difficult to convert, following the method described above, as they normally are made of a relatively soft material. The plastic saucers are, of course, easily pierced with a hot soldering iron. Sizes range from about 6 to 12 inches in diameter, with depths of 1 1/4 to 2 1/4 inches.

Chapter 8

Moss, Rocks, and Accessories

Besides the plant and the container, there are other items of little or no cost that greatly enhance the pleasure in bonsai. These include moss, rocks, and the simple accessories for displaying specimen plants.

Mosses are often used as a particularly effective ground cover in bonsai pots, the fine-textured ones suggesting a field of grass, the larger ones perhaps appearing like young evergreens beneath a tree that is only ten inches tall! Rocks serve in several roles with these potted plants: they may look like outcroppings that help balance a composition; or serve as a base that displays the entwining roots of a tree; a larger one may be a craggy bluff creating the impression of a landscape seen at a distance.

Finally, for full enjoyment of bonsai, some thought should be given to the setting. Backgrounds and accessories should be simple; they may be expensive, or devised by the owner, but they are important. Diamond rings are not presented in paper bags, and even unmounted gems are shown under favorable light against the right background.

MOSSES

Their usual position underfoot rarely attracts the attention that the beauty of mosses deserves. Unlike most wildings, they are plants easily collected at any time of the year, the season having little to do with their survival.

True mosses are plants that produce neither flowers nor seeds, although sometimes they bear capsules containing spores in bright shades of red, orange, and yellow, that seem flowerlike. They are propagated by spores, and by male and female germ cells. Species range in height from one sixteenth of an inch to twenty-four inches tall. At some seasons of the year, mosses, to some extent, are green, because they manufacture food with chlorophyll in the manner of other plants. They often are seen in their dormant condition, however, as gray, brown, or black.

Moss is not confined to a shady place, or an "acid" spot in the lawn. Varieties of moss grow almost everywhere, except in sea water. There are kinds to be found 14,000 feet high in the mountains of Colorado, on the sands of the Atlantic seashore, in deep evergreen forest shade of the Northwest, and on rocks exposed to the blazing sun in the South. Sphagnum moss is a notable type that thrives in fresh water. In this country the forests of the West Coast have more and bigger mosses than any place on the continent. Very few grow naturally in the tallgrass prairies and the shortgrass plains in the middle of the country. But in the East there are many kinds. A short climb up the side of a ravine in the Appalachians may disclose various types, from liverworts at the streamside to the types better adapted to drier conditions at the higher elevations. Low-growing and enduring species often are found in the city, growing in cracks in the pavement. Mosses may form extensive carpets, grow as small tight-knit colonies sitting loosely on the surface of the soil, or appear attached tightly to rock or wood. Close inspection will show that foliage forms vary widely. In addition to the ones that are so small and fine that they appear almost as a smooth green mat, there are others that are cordlike, growing upright or creeping, or a pattern may develop like fern fronds; some kinds assume a structure that suggests the silhouette of a young evergreen tree.

Many plants called moss are not members of the clan, and most of these are of little use to the bonsai collector. Flowering mosses of the pine barrens of New Jersey and southward, belong to the flowering plant kingdom. Arenarias and kindred plants that bloom have root systems too competitive to be used safely with bonsai, except in rare cases. Spanish moss hanging from the trees in the Deep South and Florida are bromeliads related to the pineapple. Reindeer moss and many gray mosses of trees and rocks actually are lichens, strange mutually beneficial marriages of fungi and algae. Irish moss and other so-called mosses in sea water are algae.

COLLECTING, AND USE

Mosses do not rely on roots for moisture as do most other plants, because they can absorb moisture through all their parts. This accounts for their ability to change rapidly from a dormant to a growing state with a shift in the weather. Attachment often is a mere threadlike structure serving to hold the plants in place. Sometimes moss can be picked up as colonies that seem to have no hold onto the earth whatsoever; in other cases it grips rocks or earth with great tenacity. Within the matted structure of roots and stems, however, there frequently seems to be at least a small amount of fine soil and sand, perhaps collected from the wind.

Transplanting moss is done easily, because it is not even necessary to keep specimens moist while in transit. Most mosses will revive when watered in their new location, or will renew growth through the spores or live cells amid the parent plants, if favorable conditions are created. Keeping mosses alive, however, is another matter. There are many kinds with unique requirements, limiting them to exact conditions, as in the case of a knothole moss found only in knotholes and forks of deciduous trees, especially maples. In one case, I found a particularly beautiful moss growing as colonies in the charcoal remains of a long-dead campfire. The conditions where mosses are found are not always exact guides to their needs. In another case, I found a moss in a large carpeted growth on rocks, where running water passed through and over it much of the year. It proved as adaptable as the moss from the charcoal as covering for soil in a bonsai pot.

The low mosses most useful for bonsai thrive, usually, on a fine soil. This is probably one of the reasons the Japanese finish their repotting operations by sifting such a soil on the surface. For immediate effect, a thin layer of moss may be pressed in place over the whole surface. If another effect is wanted, or if moss is in short supply, small patches can be inserted in various spots. The faster creeping kinds will soon create a cover. Another common practice is this: first, dry the moss, then rub it—tops, roots, and dirt clinging to it—through a coarse screen; second, spread this over the soil in the pot, press lightly and water gently with a fog spray. Within a month or so an adapted species in the right season will produce a green carpet.

There is division of opinion among bonsai hobbyists in this country as to the advisability of using moss as a ground cover. A few growers think that a heavy growth smothers the roots of the tree, and they either limit the use of moss, or remove it when the growth becomes thick. Under my conditions moss has proved helpful, without discernible drawbacks. It is a useful ground cover, preventing soil compaction that tends to follow repeated waterings, especially with the clay soils that I employ. Some of the most beautiful growths come from a seeding of powdered dry moss, but for immediate results transplanting is the way. I use a small mason's trowel for cutting a thin slice of soil with the moss.

Moss species vary so greatly in their habits that it is impractical to generalize on what to expect of them. During hot, dry weather in many areas, the varieties common there lapse into dormancy, even if kept watered. In the Southwest, where the summers are dry and hot, a common practice for growers is to remove the moss and store it, perhaps in jars, until the next cool season. Other kinds of moss native to other sections will remain green despite cold or heat, if kept moist. Many mosses turn other colors when dormant, while some kinds remain a dull green, even when totally dry. One of the collateral pleasures of bonsai growing is in collecting different kinds of mosses, in learning their characteristics, and in discovering for yourself the especially beautiful ones.

ROCKS

It isn't easy to define the qualities in rocks to be used with bonsai. Bright quartzite and striking igneous formations may be specimens worthy of display by themselves, but they are not well-suited to play the secondary role of accompanists to the plant.

What do the Japanese see in a stone? An American, shopping in a Tokyo department store, heard a clue to the answer. Looking over a display of bonsai and containers, he found with them a number of rocks for sale. One, a bright, fist-size pebble was priced at the equiva-

Planting an 8-inch larch on a rock:

Figure 59. Clay rubbed on rock as base for roots. *March 16*

lent of twenty-five cents, another of similar dimensions but of considerably different appearance was marked thirty dollars.

"Why should this rock cost so much more than the other?", the American asked.

The Japanese clerk smiled. Pointing to the high-priced item, he said, "That one has character."

Figure 60. Plant roots adjusted to cover side of rock.

Figure 61. Rubber pad protects roots from wire used to tie them securely in place.

Figure 62. Moss placed on surface
after soil is firmed around roots.

Figure 63. Healthy growth is
evident. *March 26*

Figure 64. First training by wiring.

Figure 65. Larch now in full leaf.
April 15

For the Japanese, rocks have varied connotations, many of them meaningless to Occidentals. In their country, rocks from certain districts are famous for their coloring and texture, and are displayed on special stands, much in the manner of bonsai. Another kind is "landscape" stone, that suggests the profile of a mountain or other natural feature and may be shown in basins of water or sand. The sermons to be seen in stones in this country are up to the individual, but there is evidence of appreciation. Frank Lloyd Wright, among others, has mounted stones for display as natural sculpture.

Stones that suggest greater proportions than their actual size would seem to fall in the class suitable for bonsai use. A round pebble looks just like what it is—a pebble. But a formation that suggests that it is merely the outcropping of a much larger mass beneath the ground is another matter. Pebbles, water-washed river gravel and shattered decaying stone—all of these I have seen used as ground covers, in various ways, with good effect. But bright stone chips compel too much attention to themselves, and collections of different kinds of rocks are unnatural.

Two types of stones particularly are useful. One is low or flattish, for placement near the trunk of a tree or under its exposed roots. The other is larger and tall, preferably with hollows, a seamed surface, or a shoulder for plants growing high above the ground line of the tray-pot. An easy way to create a stable base for such a rock, if it is concealed in soil or sand, is described in Chapter 14.

ACCESSORIES FOR DISPLAY

Aids to the effective display of bonsai do not include brightly colored figures, vehicles, bridges, or pagodas, all of which tend to be distractions. Occasionally, the Japanese use small bronze or uncolored wooden figures or other objects that are in scale, especially when these articles have a seasonal meaning in their country. The difference between them and the colorful tourist toys is the difference between the objects in a museum and in a waxworks.

Essential to display are an uncomplicated background and proper lighting. A special base for the container may contribute, but is not considered essential in this country, except in the case of cascade types. The same bases widely used today for flower arrangements are adaptable to bonsai. These may be slabs of plain or polished wood cut crosswise to reveal the grain and the natural trunk form. A black

Figure 66. Miniature bonsai displayed on a multilevel table.

or dark-colored stand with plain or carved legs or a scroll base may be suitable. A raftlike arrangement of small bamboo canes bound together is inexpensive and especially in keeping with summer displays. A rather high stand is necessary for cascades, and the Japanese often use naturally twisted root growths, polished, in dark brown or black, that have been made into stands. For miniature bonsai, multilevel tables are particularly effective.

Indoors, a plain wall of neutral shade is in keeping with any type of bonsai. By controlling the light, it is possible to make such a wall light in tone to silhouette the structure of the bonsai by illuminating it with a concealed lamp behind the plant, below, or to one side. Or a spotlight can be utilized, if it is not too dramatic, to show the delicate foliage or flowers, leaving the background in shadow.

For a background the Japanese often use a screen, either the folding type or one mounted on legs. White paper is considered proper for displaying all types, gold especially for pines, and sometimes silver for deciduous plants.

Outdoors bonsai look well against a bamboo or wood screen, or in this country, plain panels made of more permanent materials, such as masonite, plastic, and asbestos board. We have found in our garden that even plants in training deserve a simple background formed by a reed or bamboo screen. Otherwise, these small plants seem insignificant against the greater scale of proportions and contrasts in the out-of-doors. Placing a specimen before such a plain background, where it is back-lit by sunlight at certain times of the day, makes an especially beautiful display of certain foliage types.

PART III
ENJOYABLE RESULTS
QUICKLY ACHIEVED

Chapter 9

Guidelines

The quality of bonsai that suggests to the viewer that he is seeing an element of landscape is an illusion of size, created by the proportions of the plant, aided by the setting. Training a plant to assume the characteristics of maturity and old age, as seen in trees, is a strong factor contributing to the illusion. What plant to choose, which branch to cut away, which one to curve by wiring—these are a few of the questions that must be answered by those who would create bonsai.

For the Japanese there are traditional forms clearly understood through long familiarity, so that in their country a relatively simple gardener can develop what would appear to a Westerner a work of art. In our country usually it will require a conscious effort for most of us to understand the means and the objectives, although for the Japanese and the American alike the primary inspiration is the same—trees themselves. This chapter contains some of the guidelines that may help the beginner to create bonsai—reminders of the characteristics of large and ancient trees to be sought; the characteristics of saplings and youth to be avoided; the habits of growth that produce these traits; and a few of the preferences followed by some Japanese bonsaimen. With these factors and the objectives in mind, the hand of the bonsai grower will be guided in the selection of the plant, in its training and in its maintenance.

While superficial reaction to a bonsai may be that here is a huge tree re-created in miniature, such is not the case. Lines of a bonsai with relatively few branches, twigs, and leaves suggest the large tree in the same manner that a few deft strokes of an artist bring clearly to mind a remembered image. Full detail, as in a photograph or a large painting, is not needed and, indeed, would be difficult to achieve in such limited space. What we seek is *resemblance*, of the kind to be found in the relatively few character lines the caricaturist employs so

". . . the patterns of our own native trees."

Figure 67. Live oaks on the Atlantic coast of Georgia.

Figure 68. Monterey cypress facing the Pacific in California.

Figure 69. An oak in Tennessee.

effectively. We seek the simplification found in caricature, rather than the exaggeration that we associate with that art, although it would seem that nature herself has already conceived of every possible fantastic tree form.

If the tradition of bonsai is followed, we avoid the exaggeration that becomes stylized and artificial; our efforts will not be to create a plant that looks like a bonsai, but a bonsai that looks like a tree. The Japanese themselves reacted to what they considered artificiality in Chinese potted trees and went on to develop their own modern school of bonsai. We certainly can profit from a study of their results, at exhibits and through photographs. More readily accessible to most of us, however, are the patterns of our own native trees. Examples of a few are shown in Figures 67, 68, 69, 70, and 71.

The image of a tree evokes a variety of responses in the observer—perhaps the remembrance of shelter from sun, the sound of rustling leaves, the scent of mountain air, the colors of autumn. Admiration is aroused for old trees, scarred and battered by the elements, yet somehow standing austerity without complaint. The result may be an image of old age with majestic grace.

But admiration for an old tree is not the only sentiment evoked in those who know bonsai. Some viewers may see an abstract pattern, the counterpoint of music, the grace and motion of a dancer. Admiration for old trees, however, is a reaction well understood by Americans, and a study of trees is a good introduction to bonsai. At one time, I made a number of photographs of trees, some of them selected to illustrate the point that some do *not* grow old gracefully. To my surprise, many persons looking at these pictures showed admiration for the ill-shaped veterans in about the same degree as to the other old trees that created a picture that might be said to have good composition. It was not that the difference in composition was not understood; it was that old trees, holding fast to a shred of life, somehow represented qualities of character that aroused respect. Evidently,

". . . all trees in a seacoast location may have a common sculpturing."

Figure 70

ancient specimens transcend any rigid rules of composition or of bonsai. This seems to be the opinion, also, of the Japanese, who, in general, value old collected plants above all others.

How do trees develop these qualities in nature? The life story of trees shows youth characterized by similarities and symmetry while age is marked by individuality, and if there is balance, it is in asymmetry. There is a monotonous uniformity at the childhood and adolescent stages, not alone within a species, but from one kind to another as well. Oak, maple, sycamore, and hickory as young trees are shaped much alike; the same is true of fir, spruce, cedar, and hemlock. The character lines of the species develop with maturity of the individual tree under the influence of a particular environment.

On an average, tree growth follows this pattern: If seed falls on soil that will sustain life at least temporarily, germination comes according to the timing mechanism of the particular species—sometimes at once, sometimes after the passage of one or more winter seasons. Survival is dependent on moisture and light, so a taproot quickly penetrates downward, the top soars upward. If conditions are favorable, the leaves may be very large, sometimes two or three times the usual size of a mature tree. Just as the first below-ground growth

"Such are trees of exceptionally long life."

Figure 71. Bristlecone pine in the Rocky Mountains.

is a single taproot, so above ground the first development is a single stem that, eventually, will become known to gardeners as the leader. If the seedling is in the open, it is not long before side branches develop, normally outward or at an upward angle, to take advantage of this light and to crowd out competing vegetation; if the seedling is within the shady forest, slender upright growth is made slowly, the potential tree remaining part of the suppressed underbrush until the moment comes when some towering giant is stricken and an opportunity is offered in the sun. The form of youth, then, is either a slender sapling or a pyramidal or globular mass of foliage starting close

Figure 72. Bald cypress in Florida.

to the ground. In the latter case, it is the Christmas-tree shape of many needled evergreens, the rounded form of deciduous and broad-leaf evergreen trees or shrubs that many American gardeners attempt to keep forever adolescent.

Figure 73

The lofty wine-glass form of the American elm (shown here in Washington, D.C.), Figure 73, is repeated by the Japanese in training zelkova as bonsai, Figure 74, often less than two feet tall.

Figure 74

RULES OF GROWTH

There are general rules of tree growth that, in youth, are supported by vigor to give advantage to the instinct to achieve stature, to guide natural development of the species, and to influence reaction to adversity. These natural tree habits of growth are worthy of special note in their application to the training of bonsai. They are:

A. Trees grow at two points: (1) In the bud, where development extends the leader, branches, and twigs. (2) In the cambium layer under the bark, where a new layer of wood is formed each season (annual rings) to support the structure. Trunk and branches continue to increase in girth, even though the extent of height and spread of the tree is repeatedly reduced by natural forces or by pruning.

B. Terminal, or end buds, on the leader or branches, especially those growing upward, have first call on sap for their development. Many buds are formed that remain dormant, at the axil of each leaf (axillary buds) and in many places hidden within the stem (adventitious buds). The terminal bud apparently secretes a hormonelike substance that inhibits the development of these side buds. Destroy this bud at the end of the branch, however, and the buds immediately behind the injury spring to life.

C. The branches of a tree with the most leafage in good light grow the most. Leaves call on the root system for moisture and minerals, combine these with elements of the air and the energy of the sun by the process of photosynthesis, and in return supply the food that sustains life. The part of a tree that performs this function best gets priority.

These are the basic habits of growth that produce the characteristics of youth and leave their mark in age, varying somewhat with the

Figure 75. This 70-foot pine on Lookout Mountain near Chattanooga, Tenn., follows closely the classic lines of formal upright style of bonsai.

Figure 76. A 26-inch bonsai can seem equally large.

species and the individual. First, the single upright stem, then side branches often at an upward angle, and at the same time an altered spreading of the root system. Some species maintain a taproot or deep anchor roots, but invariably roots also soon grow outward near the surface of the ground, where there normally is a greater supply of plant food.

The process of growth in time produces its own changes, its own pruning. As upper branches develop, they shade lower ones and these losers in the competitive battle droop, die, and fall away. Branches, at a certain point on the trunk of a tree, not only do not rise with growth at this point, but actually grow earthward in *girth* and, usually, in direction, under the weight of wood and leafage. Characteristically lower branches droop in maturity, in some cases in an arching curve with an upward movement at the growing tip, in others with an almost abrupt sag at the trunk; these developments vary with the species. Below-ground growth produces a similar increased spread and increased girth of its members. Soil erosion often combines with this enlargement of roots near the surface to disclose a root structure supporting the base of the trunk.

Events in youth and vigorous middle age produce youthful reaction. Destroy the leader or the top of a tree and there is a heroic reaction to re-establish it. In the case of deciduous or broadleaf evergreen trees, adventitious buds long held for such an emergency quickly awaken to produce a rash of new upright branches. In other trees, especially many of the conifers in which buds do not remain alive in old wood, the side branches still unharmed near the damage—although previously horizontal—move upward to a vertical position.

When branches or a trunk bend sideways or downward, or for any other reason become less able to carry on healthy upward growth during the years of vigor, a common response is for adventitious buds to develop into upright branches called water sprouts. These grow rapidly, have widely spaced internodes and a few larger leaves, but once they have reached upward to sunlight, they themselves may become new trunks or major branches. Shrubs—separated from trees only by reason of a lesser stature and, sometimes, lack of a distinguishable trunk—commonly develop canes similar to water sprouts that also show little diminution of size from bottom to top. Many of these shrubs first establish themselves in modest proportions, and then as the roots develop reserve capacities, produce sprouts from the base or from the lower branching that grow upward to achieve a greater dimension. These are mentioned here, because many shrubs, even multistem types, can become effective bonsai, if trained to treelike proportions. Upright rapid growth, straight and without taper, however, is characteristic of youth in trees or of small-stature plants.

MATURITY AND OLD AGE

Height and maturity give a tree dominance, but with it comes new restraining forces. New growth must be made each year, despite the practical limits of size; the compromise is branches with shorter internodes, twiggy growth at the ends of branches, the whole tree clothed with smaller leaves. Natural pruning leaves its mark, the result of insects, shading, and other damage. In addition, the large tree eventually must bear the brunt of destructive storms. Old trees respond slowly to injury; snags and splintered trunks may never heal, although healthy growth may continue on the living parts, sometimes for many years. The capacity to grow slowly, despite injury, is one secret of the longevity of the bristlecone pine at the timberline high in the Rocky Mountains. The peril of great size has been lessened by the banyan tree, with aerial roots which descend, from place to place, to grow in the soil below, and thus to form new trunks supporting the ever-extending branches. Another adaptation with great height is the big tree redwood of California, with colossal trunk development in proportion to the amount of foliage exposed to the force of wind. Another is the weighty mass of buttressed trunk and extending roots, sometimes with their strange "knees," that rise above the normal water level, of bald cypress (*Taxodium*) that give a stable base to these trees in the southern swamps. Such are trees of exceptionally long life.

Age reveals the character of all species. The American elm, with the loss of lower limbs, develops a tall, straight bole that ramifies into a number of nearly upright branches in the well-known wineglass form; it is a favorite pattern used by Japanese bonsaimen in training zelkova, a near relative of the elm. In some species, notably spruce and fir, a stout leader bears branches that all slant downward, a structure well designed to cope with the weight of ice and snow.

Weather and time leave their special marks. Under pressure of prevailing winds, only buds on the leeward side survive, so all trees in a seacoast location may have a common sculpturing. Winter gales in the mountains, laden with sharp ice particles, can sandblast all living tissue from the windward side of trees in exposed places, leaving polished deadwood; the sheltered side may continue to live and grow.

". . . for the Japanese and the American alike the primary inspiration is . . . trees themselves."

Figure 77. Wind-swept trees.

Figure 78. Bonsai in wind-swept style.

Storms tear away or break branches. Terminal buds are destroyed, new growth takes a different direction, branches thus become gnarled or sinuous. The symmetry of youth is gone, the trunk stands forth, branches show the character of the species or are carved by the elements.

In the eastern half of the United States, the red cedar (*Juniperus virginiana*) is an example of how the lines of youth and old age are recognized at a glance. The young tree is a formal pointed oval of tight foliage, with little or no trunk exposed. With age, the trunk is seen buttressed at the base, the branches can be noted through irregular masses of leaves. On the West Coast, the rare Torrey pine is known for its sculpturing by nature. In its natural range, the Torrey pine is limited to about 3000 picturesque, gnarled specimens divided between a colony clinging to the bluffs overlooking the Pacific, just north of San Diego, and a second grove on wind-swept Santa Rosa Island off Santa Barbara. Grown from seed, in protected areas, the Torrey is just another vigorous young pine without special distinction.

GUIDELINES FROM NATURE

From this general survey of trees, we may deduce that we should strive—in our selection of plants, and in their training—to seek certain character lines and to avoid others, varying, of course, according to the species.

SEEK:

A trunk with a broad base at the roots, tapering as it ascends.

Branches well spaced, with their structure and part of the trunk revealed.

Figure 79. Engelmann's spruce sandblasted by ice particles in a high mountain pass near Denver, Colorado.

Figure 80. "Such injuries . . .
enhance the illusion that this is a
battle-scarred veteran."

Some roots on the surface of the ground, or at least suggested by the spreading base of the trunk.

Upper branches progressively shorter, ramifying more quickly in twiggage.

Lower branches directed downward or branches gnarled or sinuous. Small leaves.

AVOID:

Trunks and branches without taper.

Branches without twiggage.

Trunk and branch structure obscured by foliage.

A trunk that emerges from the ground like a post, without base or taper.

Large leaves.

PREFERENCES OF SOME JAPANESE BONSAIMEN

There are no rules of art on how to form a bonsai any more than there are on how to paint a picture, although there are traditional forms and esthetic considerations, schools of thought, and standards followed by individuals. Some of the preferences that I have heard or read are printed below. A few of these relate to the health of the plant, some to its beauty, and one, at least in part, is based on superstition. These may be of interest and need not be misleading if viewed within the frame of reference of their limitations.

PREFER:

Use of the triangle, "heaven, man, and earth"—so widely understood here in Japanese flower arrangements—in composing the placement of branches, the composition of the whole tree, trunks, branches and accessory rocks which might be used in the pot, and in the placement of bonsai in a composition for display.

Branches set closer together toward the top of the tree, preferably in groups of threes, especially in upright styles. In this case, starting at the bottom, one branch will extend to the right, the next to the left (or vice versa), the third one in back between them, or slightly above or below.

A "front" side of the tree with no branches extending forward from it to obscure the line of the trunk, except toward the very top of the tree.

At least one third of the total height of the tree revealed as trunk, especially in upright types.

In the upright style, the top of the tree leaning slightly toward the front.

In slanting styles, the lowest branch opposite to the slant of the tree.

Curved trunks and main branches with a side branch, to break the continuous line of the curve, except in the case of certain weeping trees.

The use of uneven numbers, except the number two, in group plantings. The number four is avoided as unlucky, in the same way some of us consider thirteen. (One way of writing four in Japanese is similar to the sign for death.) Preference for uneven numbers is justified, also, by the fact that it is easier to create a focal point with them than with even numbers.

USUALLY AVOID:

One branch immediately above another (a hazard to the continued health of the tree).

Division into a U near the end of a branch. (One Japanese nurseryman translates a term for these as "bothered branches.")

Parallel branching.

Several branches from one place.

Opposite branching or branches from either side of the trunk to form a crossing line or bar. (It is interesting to note that while trees in habit either are alternate or opposite branching, as they also bear leaves in an alternate or opposite position on the branch, this characteristic rarely persists in old age as a part of the over-all structure. Maples are favorite bonsai subjects, despite their opposite leaves and branching, which is suppressed by pruning. Old maples, however, do not show this trait in their structure, because in time one or the other of the opposite branches achieves dominance, the lesser one dies and falls away. Opposite branching, then, is a juvenile trait to be avoided.)

Any evidence of treatment by man. (Stubbed branches and any suggestion that a tree has been topped or cut off short, is unacceptable. Even the place where a branch has been neatly sawn away is frowned on until the spot heals. Markings on the trunk where this healing has occurred can add to the beauty of the trunk, but evidence of the pruning saw is anathema. If a scar cannot be avoided, a stub may be left that is cut and carved to suggest that it was broken by natural forces. Such injuries, with deadwood remaining, enhance the illusion that this is a battle-scarred veteran. Even heart rot is preferable to the mark of the pruner.)

Chapter 10

Step One, Step Two

The first step in creation of bonsai is selection of the plant and decision as to its ultimate form. Although this latter judgment is not irrevocable, it is helpful in the beginning to see the direction of development both to guide the selection and to plan for training.

The second step is the initial period of training. If there is still a secret to bonsai, it is in overlooking the fact that the training period usually is used to *speed* the transformation of a plant to bonsai. If there is a major stumbling block for Americans who are interested in bonsai but discouraged by the time factor, it is this oversight, combined with a failure to see how to exploit the immediate display potentials of many plants while they are in training.

SELECTION

In judging plants, the Japanese have a saying "first the trunk, second the branches, third the roots." In hunting for plant material for bonsai, we might usefully modify this at the selection stage: "first the leaves, second the trunk, third the branches, and fourth the roots."

Leaf size is important in achieving the illusion of bonsai, and the reduction practical in training is usually applicable equally to those leaves already naturally small as to the larger ones. Sometimes growers use plants with larger leaves, especially the kinds with compound structures that display smaller subdivisions as leaflets, but this is the exception rather than a useful rule. Bonsai treatment rarely reduces the size of flowers and fruit, so if this is important in the final result, varieties with smaller blossoms and fruits should be chosen.

The first survey of potential bonsai, then, should concentrate attention on plants with small leaves.

The second should be to appraise the trunk for taper and interesting form. It is fair to say that without a worthwhile trunk there is no immediate potential for bonsai.

The third should be a study of the placement of branches on the trunk. One should attempt to decide which side should be the front of the plant. Since in many instances the total height of the plant will be reduced, perhaps drastically, it is important that vigorous branches are located low on the trunk.

Finally, examination should be made of the root structure at the base of the trunk. If other factors are favorable, the beginner may feel justified in ignoring this point, especially since it is difficult to be sure of the spread and placement of roots when examining nursery plants or those growing in the ground. But roots should not be considered last in importance. Often they make a contribution of such significance that they are the margin of difference between a mediocre bonsai and an outstanding one. In fact, I agree with those expert growers like James R. Raker that after the first glance eliminates the obviously unsuitable plants, this vital base of the trunk should be considered first. Trunks and branches may be altered or developed, but little can be done with older plants which do not have sufficient root splay or a balanced supporting root structure.

Plants that are irregular in form, that are gnarled or twisted, will catch the eye of the bonsai hunter. They often are to be found in the discard area of a nursery, set aside as of less value by the nurseryman who tries mainly for symmetrical plants. To him these discards may seem deformed. But to the creator of bonsai, qualities suggesting strength and beauty are sought in these maverick individuals which have escaped regimentation. The eye searching for traditional bonsai looks for beauty of character, never ugliness or deformity. In the tradition of bonsai, even a plant that suggests a tree shattered by storms, parts of it reduced to deadwood bleached by the weather, assumes the role of the central figure in a tragedy, arousing admiration in the viewer, not pity.

Perhaps some beginners with bonsai see first only those qualities that are picturesque or that look Japanese. But these are superficialities. The Japanese stress the poetic qualities to be found in nature, and when occasionally they try to express in words their reactions to a plant, they may use such terms as "forceful," "rugged and grand," "simple and refined." They may say a plant is "gentle and well formed," "masculine," or has "gracefulness." Although some bonsai created by the Japanese approach the fantastic, I have never seen specimens or photographs of them that arouse pity.

Esthetically, within the art form of bonsai, I can see no reason why an American artist should not create an American version of bonsai that is shocking or ugly, arousing in the viewer pain, hatred, or horror. I can, in fact, envisage a miniature tree depicting the agony and deformity of a street tree pruned to permit the passage of overhead wires. But up to now, this art of the Japanese does not seem to include such an aim.

DECISION ON FORM

The form sought for each individual bonsai should be determined through agreement between the grower and the plant itself. No poetic concept is implied here, although the mystically inclined person might consider such intercommunication a kind of Zen philosophy. Perhaps the hardheaded will think of it as the practical and more rapid route to effective results. These decisions cannot be made in a book. Some of the lines of communication from the plant that could be explored, however, include:

A straight massive trunk with pronounced taper suggests the possibility of an upright forest giant; a graceful trunk might be adapted to a slanting style as a single specimen, or the major element with one or two additional trees of similar form but lesser stature in a group planting; side branching, or nearly procumbent trunk, a windswept specimen, or a cascading tree form. Natural characteristics of the species are always in keeping with the individual; maples that commonly develop attractive surface roots can be trained with this feature in mind.

Whether the creator of bonsai sits cross-legged, sipping hot tea, or reclines in a lawn chair with his beverage iced, much pleasant time can be spent seeking inspiration from the plant. Often the message is not clear, at least in my experience; somehow the plant attracts, but no clear plan comes to mind. Sometimes characters in a book seem to take charge of the writer, paintings to direct the stroke of the painter; so it is with bonsai. And with the added dimension in bonsai of time and change, sometimes a plant will serve first in one capacity, then be transferred to another role.

In visualizing plans for bonsai I have employed such aids as sketches and photographs. It is easy to combine these means by placing tracing paper on top of the photographic print and sketching a variety of alterations on the semitransparent sheets. This affords an opportunity to see changes without being committed to any permanent alteration wrought by pruning or wiring. Several sketches by James R. Raker, of Playa del Rey, Los Angeles, California, are included in this book, with photographs of nursery plants in the early stages of their conversion to a bonsai kind of training and potting. Such older plants already have established characteristics that limit practical alterations, but, as Raker pointed out to me, even within these limitations, the sketches he made are not the only, nor necessarily the best, plans for the plants involved. I do believe these sketches represent what a perceptive and skilled bonsai grower can see in ordinary nursery stock, and they illustrate how this method can help in developing plans for training.

The first example is of a small cotoneaster growing in a gallon nursery can, selected because of its small, colorful autumn leaves and berries and interesting trunk. (Figures 81, 82, 83, 84, and 85.) In a matter of minutes, repotting and pruning changed the proportions. Wiring created better branch placement. Since this repotting was done just before winter, I did not cut back the roots sharply, because plants severely pruned and in small pots sometimes are killed by cold weather. Plans for this plant included cleaning the roots of the peat-moss-and-sand mixture, in which they were growing, and repotting in a soil for bonsai the next spring. Then, according to the sketch, pruning for better balance, smoothing the stub on the trunk with a wood-carving tool, and, during the growing season, developing a secondary branch to complete the composition.

Figure 81. Small cotoneaster in 1-gallon nursery can.

Figure 82. Removed from container, the root ball reduced.

Figure 83. Repotted and pruned.

Figure 84. Branch position controlled by wiring.

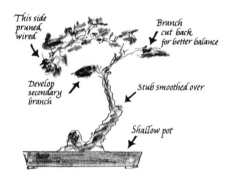

Figure 85. Drawing suggests further development.

JAMES R. RAKER

Another ordinary nursery plant is shown in Figures 86, 87, 88, and 89, as an example of the whims of training in bonsai style. The plant was a nursery-grown tamarisk in a gallon can, at first, with a bristle of new growth the result of pruning by the nurseryman the year before. Removal of the top section of the main shoot with a slanting cut, and wiring the side branch to take its place, gave some suggestion of taper to the trunk. The root ball of earth was reduced from both top and bottom, and the plant put in a shallow pot with the trunk in an inclined position. The rock was put in place primarily to hold down the roots that tended to rise above the new soil level on that side. A sheet of growing moss also helped cover the roots that otherwise might have been harmed by being immediately exposed. After repotting was completed, slender florist wire was used to curve the branches. As new growth began in spring, the plant seemed interesting, so it was transferred to a Japanese pot, and because the two containers were about the same size, hazard in doing so, during this active growing period, was eliminated. The result was a stylized plant. Removal of the leading branch created more of the impression of a wind-blown tree, but then the pot became noticeably too large and heavy for good proportions.

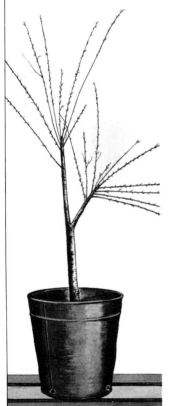

Figure 86. March 25—Drawing shows how tamarisk looked in nursery can.

Figure 87. After pruning, wiring, and repotting.

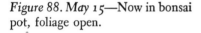

Figure 88. May 15—Now in bonsai pot, foliage open.

Figure 89. The long leading branch removed.

This tamarisk is not an example of a serious effort to create bonsai, but it suggests the kind of bonsai techniques that can be adapted to ordinary plants found almost everywhere. A projection of the series of photographs of this tamarisk, over a period of two or three seasons, could also illustrate a significant point about training and care of bonsai: if this plant were kept in a large container, or returned to a ground bed and allowed considerable leaf and branch growth, the trunk would develop greater girth, and a better branch structure could be trained in a shorter time. On the other hand, if this plant were repotted in a container of minimum size, the trunk would remain almost stationary, and branches would develop more slowly. Such results the reader already may have inferred from the rules of plant growth described in the last chapter.

THE START OF TRAINING

The exciting time with bonsai is the period of development, when qualities in a plant are perceived, a new role for it planned, and often drastic changes undertaken. The owner who purchases a fine bonsai has the pride of possession and the pleasure its care may afford; those who train bonsai know some of the joys of creation as well. Although there are similarities in the treatment of finished bonsai and of plants in training, there also are significant differences.

The purpose of training is to adapt a plant with some of the desired characteristics to bonsai culture, or to *hasten* the development of such characteristics. The first step in the training period will be dictated by the time of year, the source and condition of the plant, and whether extensive further development is indicated.

In deciding which course to follow at the beginning, the grower should keep in mind one distinction between finished bonsai and other potted plants in general—and some bonsai-in-training in particular. The distinction is this: finished bonsai in pots of minimum size for display make very slow growth; girth of trunk and branches increases very little. The further training given such plants is more a matter of refinement, in most cases, than development. Plants which have achieved the stature of bonsai, in consequence, do not as a general rule follow the usual progressive steps of other pot plants in moving from smaller to larger containers. In other words, a small bonsai rarely becomes a medium-size bonsai and then, finally, a large bonsai. The prospect for many bonsai is to remain in the same size display pot for the length of their lives. The exceptions to this, where very slow increase in size is permitted and how plants are kept healthy under these restraints, are explained in the latter part of this book.

Plants in training requiring further development, then, obviously should not be hurried into the smallest possible container. In fact, in many cases they are better off if not planted in containers at first. It is common practice for Japanese bonsaimen to grow many of their plants in the ground in the initial stage of development, and the same practice is followed by bonsai hobbyists in this country. This is a chance to "fatten up" lean, young specimens, and to encourage healthy redevelopment of older plants.

As one grower here pointed out to me, the place for optimum growth of a plant usually is in the ground. The next-best substitute is a large wooden box on the ground. Less favorable is the same box raised above the ground. This progression goes through smaller containers to a small porous pot on a bench or table as the least favorable environment for vigorous growth. His reasoning is this: In addition to offering greater area for root development, the ground bed is a place where the extremes of climate, of temperature and moisture are moderated; the wooden container is somewhat moisture retentive, and on the ground the "climate" is usually better; in a raised position the extremes from flood, when the plant is watered, to a comparative drought a few hours later, tend to prevail, and the temperature and humidity range is greater.

A "ground bed" for bonsai may be an extensive nursery area or a small corner of the garden. The basic requirements are sun, good drainage, and an average garden soil. Some means of shading, at least part of the time, with lath panels or the like, can be of value. Having water close at hand is a great convenience for the grower. For those without garden space, large containers will serve if the plants are given the proper attention.

All plants that need considerable growth before conversion to bonsai are not started in ground beds, however. Some kinds, especially vigorous varieties that require constant training, are kept in containers of varying sizes from the time they are seedlings. Others are potted early in their training as a more convenient means of restraining growth. And there is considerable advantage—to the grower—of having plants in larger containers in a raised position, where it is more convenient to give them frequent attention. In particular this appeals to American growers who are averse to the physical strain of "stoop" labor. A balancing factor is that a plant given good care in a less-than-ideal location may be better off than a neglected one with optimum growing conditions.

We might usefully divide plants at the beginning of training into three groups:

First, are the older plants that already have adequate trunk development and a good root system. These are generally found among older nursery-grown and well-rooted collected plants, and they may prove decorative even in the early stages of training. The process of adapting them to bonsai is largely a matter of pruning—below ground to create a compact root system that can be potted down by stages to a small container—above ground to establish the right proportions and to develop a better branch and twig structure. The first planting of these specimens usually is in containers or boxes that are a little larger than planned for ultimately.

Second, are those plants requiring drastic change to bonsai, including collected plants with poor root systems, and others undergoing "major surgery," such as strenuous trunk bending with braces, vises, and the like. The most favorable conditions for recuperation, of a ground bed or a large box, are indicated.

Third, are the young plants that can be greatly improved, usually in a season or two, by what might be called a period of pre-bonsai training. Plants with some of the desired characteristics, but still in need of considerable growth, are in this group. Also the youngsters you may have started at home by the methods described in Chapter 6. The treatment of these plants is much like that accorded nursery plants in general, but with special attention to developing such qualities as a balanced root system and low branching, which are of importance in plants for bonsai. The longer the bonsai hobbyist seeks the "perfect" older plant at nurseries and in the wild, the more he may see the value of this slower, but important, pre-bonsai period that he can control. Plants in this class may be grown for a time in individual pots, in ground beds, or in large, shallow boxes called "flats."

More detailed information on these procedures and some of the problems with these three classes of plants will be found in the next three chapters.

Chapter 11

Potting-Soil Mixtures

Potting bonsai deserves special attention not because it is a difficult or complicated operation—reading about it will take more time than the job itself—but because what is done at this stage has a great bearing on the future health of the plant, its development as bonsai, and the amount of attention it will require. The below-ground treatment of the roots is, in every way, as significant as the more obvious aboveground training of the plant.

The demands on the potting soil used for bonsai are considerably greater than for the ordinary houseplant or nursery plant, as anyone soon finds out who grows these small plants in shallow containers exposed to the drying action of wind and sun. The Japanese have developed methods of potting and of combining soils that deserve special consideration.

If there is a bewildering element in this subject of potting, it is in the wide variations in the soil mixtures that are strongly endorsed. Growers in Japan alter the mixture not only for different kinds of plants, but also for those in training and for finished plants. They even change the consistency of the soil at different levels in the container. American growers with whom I have had contact tend to standardize their potting mixtures to a greater extent, avoiding the complicated variations that some of the Japanese recommend. But growers here usually have a preferred formula, and many of them are insistent on the rightness of a particular way.

Observation of bonsai culture in this country shows success with soils that vary tremendously. Some hobbyists use a standard mixture of equal parts loam soil, peat moss, and sand. Others use such combinations as the following: sandy subsoil clay three parts, leafmold one part; pulverized subsoil and limestone equal parts, plus 10 per cent leafmold; compost three parts, peat moss two parts, sand one part.

If success can be achieved by Japanese bonsaimen following somewhat diverse paths, and by their American counterparts in such disagreement, it might seem logical to conclude that the kind of potting soil is of little importance. This is not true. The point is that almost *any recommended potting mixture can be used if the qualifying factors of care and climate are the same as for the one who has successfully used it.* Plants can be grown in sand if feeding and watering are carefully attended to, although in full sun this might mean watering ten times a day. In a different potting soil the same plant might be given sufficient moisture by once-a-day attention.

For the beginner, the meaning is this: If you know a successful grower in your area, you may confidently follow his potting methods if you have the same kind of plants and soil, and can give them similar care. For other growers without such a local example, a more careful analysis of plant needs and the causes and effects of differing soils is worth patient investigation and experimentation. No formula for potting soil can prevent damage or loss from prolonged neglect, but some combinations demand less skill in watering and somewhat less frequent attention.

Gardeners in most places in the world modify natural soils to create potting mixtures better adapted to the needs of plants with roots unnaturally confined. Soil provides the anchorage for the roots, is the principal source of moisture and the small amount of mineral nutrients that are required. In addition, the soil must be porous enough to permit roots to penetrate and to allow the movement of air, as well as water, between its particles. Under pot culture, there is a tendency for soil to become more compact with repeated heavy waterings and with the accumulation of roots. To forestall or delay the development of this unhealthy condition, potting soils are made more porous by adding to natural soil varying amounts of such materials as sand and organic matter or humus. Fertility also may be increased by adding fertilizers, but with fully soluble fertilizers at hand for application whenever needed, the main qualities needed are the proper porosity and an adequate moisture-retentive ability. In natural soils, the porosity and the ability to retain moisture vary tremendously, according to the type.

NATURAL SOILS

The separate mineral elements that make up natural soils range from sand, the coarsest, to clay, the finest. Clay is so fine (particles below .002 millimeters) that water will penetrate it at a rate of only one foot a day, while sand (.05 to 1. millimeters) is so porous water will pass through 1500 feet of it in the same time. As might be expected, sand dries out quickly, while clay hangs onto moisture for a long time. Roots grow well in sand, if frequently supplied with the right amount of moisture, which accounts for the generous use of sand in mixtures for seedlings and cuttings. Roots find compact clay inhospitable, so grow slowly in it or perish, if it is poorly drained.

It is unusual to find either clay or sand in pure deposits. Natural soils are mixtures of materials of many sizes, created by such actions as the settlings of moving water as silt, deposits by the winds as loess, the accumulations of organic matter and minerals on forest floors, or the result of many other forces. These mixtures, which range somewhere between pure sand and pure clay, we call loam.

Loam is a combination of many-size particles. If most of these are very fine, it is called a clay loam. If of a medium-fine size, a silt loam. If coarse, a sandy loam. It is interesting to note that sandy soils are called "light," while clay soils are "heavy," although the actual weight of the material did not earn the names for them. Sandy loams are loose, so are easily plowed with a "light" team; clay loams are tight and offer considerable resistance to the plow, so require a "heavy" team (or tractor).

The granular texture of a soil is not dependent entirely on the size of the mineral particles. Even clay soils, if properly treated—in "good tilth," as the farmer would say—have a granular structure, due to the fact that fine particles of clay form small clumps, with spaces between for the movement of air and water. The roots of plants require both air and water, and a good soil has a high percentage of air-water space in relation to its solid elements.

We usually think of loam as containing humus, a product of decaying vegetation and other organic matter. This organic substance adds to the fertility of the soil, soaks up large quantities of water, thereby making a sandy soil more moisture retentive; it increases porosity, thereby making a clay loam more open to the penetration of air, water, and roots. Humus sounds like the panacea for all soil ills, but used in high concentrations or alone, it is not. Gardeners have found that, under certain climate conditions, organic materials like peat moss or peat humus alternately can stay too wet too long, and then when dry, become actually water repellent.

The ideal soil would have the good qualities of the extremes—the structural porosity of sand, the water-retaining ability of clay—without the undesirable fast-drying characteristic of the former, or the inhospitable density of the latter. If we could create such a soil, and add the right amount of humus, then presto, we would have the perfect potting soil. It sounds magical and unattainable, but the Japanese have gone a long way toward attaining this ideal. How? By following two practices that are not generally known in this country.

First, they sieve their potting soils, retaining several granular sizes and—especially in the case of clay soils—they throw away the finest part. Second, they pot with dry soil. The theory is that the inclusion of the dusty part of fine soil would fill up pore space, and that damp potting soil containing clay would lose much of its porosity if firmly packed into the pot. Dry soil can be tamped around the roots without destroying its granular structure. The tiny granules of clay act as reservoirs of moisture, and between them are the air-water spaces and the other materials of the potting mixture, the sand and humus.

All successful bonsai growers in this country do not follow these practices, but if clay soils are used, it is indicated. In cool, humid areas, where droughts are infrequent, moisture-retentive soil is not so important. And, of course, if watering is attended to frequently enough, a fairly light soil will serve almost anywhere.

PREPARING SOIL

In order to prepare sieved bonsai soil, wire sieves of several mesh sizes are required, plus suitable containers for mixing and storing. Some Japanese bonsaimen use seven grades of sieves, from three to thirty-five wires per inch, and a number of hobbyists here use this kind of imported kit. The seven sieves nest together, the coarsest at the top, the finest at the bottom. Soil introduced at the top is thus graded by size as it passes through the various sieves. What comes from the bottom is discarded.

At the other extreme are some growers here who merely use two sieves, the coarse one has three or four wires to the inch, the bottom one ordinary window screening, which has fourteen or fifteen wires to the inch. This seems satisfactory, at least for medium and larger pots, and I used this system at first. For smaller, shallow pots, perhaps some of the finer granules lost through the window screening would be valuable. For the coarsest screen, one-fourth-inch mesh wire called "hardware cloth" is available at most hardware stores. Or, expanded metal lath will serve, and this is handled by building-supply firms.

Presently, I use four screens of mesh sizes 1/4 inch, 1/8 inch, 1/16 inch, and 1/32 inch. The last one listed is a fine grade that may be difficult to find, except from companies that specialize in "wire cloth" or woven-wire screens.

In practice I follow this procedure—cited here not as ideal, but perhaps as fairly typical of amateur growers: Clay soil dug from a field

Figure 90. Coarse, granular soil for use in the bottom of bonsai pots.

Figure 91. Finer, sifted mixture for the main potting soil.

I spread in thin layers in boxes, which are stored for a few days in a shed until the clay is quite dry. The sieves I made from 1×4 lumber, cut to a size to permit a piece of screen wire one foot square to be conveniently stapled in place to form the bottom of an open box. The four sieves are set, one upon another, in a stack within a somewhat larger box. Dry clods of clay are put in a shallow tub, where they are crushed to a finer consistency. The material is sieved by rubbing and shaking it through the four screened boxes. What emerges at the bottom I throw on the compost pile. Except for the very large lumps, which are again crushed, I save what remains on top of the 1/4-inch screen for use in the bottom of deep pots. In like manner, the soil on top of the 1/8-inch screen is set aside for bottom-soil mixtures. Then, the soils from the top of the 1/16- and 1/32-inch screens are mixed together and stored for use in the main potting-soil mixture.

If all ingredients used in the potting are sieved to these different sizes, a rather large number of containers for storage are needed. For small amounts, I find plastic bags convenient, because the contents can be seen through the bag, so labeling is not required. It hardly seems necessary to sieve sand and some humus materials that are used, but some growers do this, also. Sieving is most important for the clay soils, and for the loam.

BASIC INGREDIENTS

The basic ingredients for a potting soil are: (1) Soil—whether it be loam topsoil or subsoil clay. (2) Humus, such as leafmold, compost, or peat moss. (3) Granular material, such as sand.

Sand is available from hardware stores and building-supply dealers. The kind used for mixing concrete, sometimes called "sharp sand," should be used. Or, sand from stream beds that frequently includes silt can be substituted. Avoid seashore sand, which is salty.

Humus, in many forms, is to be found at stores or nurseries that supply gardeners. Peat moss is a widely available source of humus. It is sold in dry, compressed bales, or in a somewhat moist condition in plastic-lined bags. The latter may actually be peat humus, a somewhat decayed form of peat moss, and some kinds contain considerable sand. Peat mosses may be almost neutral or strongly acid. Other humus sources include sphagnum moss, leafmold, ground bark, sugarcane pith, and composted manures. Dried manures are sold as fertilizer, but supply humus, also.

Loam topsoil may be considered anything that serves as the upper level of soil in a garden (or field) that is capable of producing reasonably good crops of flowers or vegetables. It varies greatly from Tennessee to Oregon, and frequently from one garden to another in the same suburban block.

Clay is the one ingredient that may not be available close at hand to gardeners in all parts of this country. Frequently it is found in greater quantities in the subsoil that lies below the loam. Popular opinion to the contrary, subsoil is not necessarily poorer in nutrients than some loams. Almost always, it contains less humus, less nitrogen, and tends to be less granular than topsoil, but it may be rich in phosphates, potash, and vital trace minerals. Sometimes, the only places clay can be found, in areas of sandy soil, are the beds of ponds or slow-moving streams.

Two practical tests may be used to gauge the clay. Where clay predominates, the moist soil is quite plastic, forms sticky balls between the fingers, dries to hard clods. Silt with some clay is less plastic, feels floury between the fingers, crumbles and is dusty when dry. Even a small amount of sand is noticeable in a soil, because it feels gritty. If there is much sand, however, the soil will not hold a shape readily, even when pressed together when wet, and it dries quickly and falls apart.

A second way to test for the ingredients is to mix a sample of soil in water, shaking it thoroughly for several minutes in a bottle. Place the bottle aside and the process of settling will soon give some indication of the proportions. The sand will settle to the bottom quickly; silt forms the next layer and, finally, the clay the upper layer, although this may require a day. Humus material, if present, may be found in the silt or clay, or if only partially decayed, it may float.

Despite the confusing variables, the basic formula for a potting mixture is SOIL plus SAND plus HUMUS, and—sometimes—plus fertilizer. The proportions of the ingredients should be based on the expected demands of the climate and the needs of the plant, related to amendments required by nature of the basic soil available.

In the cool, humid coastal climate zones of the Northeast and Northwest, a potting soil with perfect drainage is imperative, but the moisture-retentive quality of clay is of lesser importance. For many areas, such as my home in Tennessee, where occasionally there are prolonged rains in some seasons and extended periods of drought at other times, there is a need for both good drainage and moisture retention. Amendments to environment, other than potting soil, are necessary to meet some of the emergency periods of extreme weather, but good potting soil helps. It is the extremes rather than the average weather that injures or kills plants, and the plant grower needs to be prepared as best he may.

If climate and anticipated care indicate that it is desirable to include clay in the potting mixture, then the proportions will depend on what kind of natural topsoil is available. If the soil is sandy, then more clay and less sand would be suggested; if a clay loam, less or no clay and more sand. For instance, in compounding an average potting soil, I use as the loam mixture one part good clay loam, plus two parts red subsoil clay; to three parts of this mixture are added two parts sand and one part humus, the latter usually peat moss, leafmold, or compost. If my loam mixture were sandy, I probably would use only one part sand.

TWO GRANULAR GRADES

To assure perfect drainage and encourage healthy root growth, it is wise to follow the Japanese practice of using a coarser soil mixture below the roots and, sometimes, around the sides of the pot. Sieving, then, should produce at least two grades of granular materials.

Among the exceptions to the rule that bonsai need porous soil and good drainage are the cypresses (Taxodium) *that grow in our southern swamps. Here a small pond cypress starts its training planted on a rock. This plant is described in Chapter 14.*

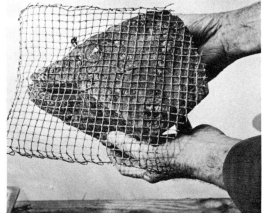

Figure 92. Wired specimen ready for repotting.

Figure 93. Galvanized-wire mesh to hold the soil is attached to the stone with epoxy glue.

Figure 94. The rock and the container.

Figure 95. May 15—As leaves develop.

Figure 96. July 1—The first summer.

Of the many potting-soil ingredients that are widely available, the following are grouped as rough equivalents as an example of possible combinations:

Main Potting-Soil Mixture
(the finer grade for use around the roots)

*LOAM MIXTURE	+	SAND	+	*HUMUS
Sandy loam or				leafmold or
silt loam or				peat moss or
clay loam				peat humus or
and/or				milled sphagnum moss
clay				or compost

* The soil and humus material that remains above the 1/16- and 1/32-inch mesh sieves.

Bottom Potting-Soil Mixture
(the coarser grade for use below the roots)

*LOAM MIXTURE	+	SAND	+	*HUMUS
Loam		and/or		leafmold or
and/or		perlite or		peat moss or
clay		granite poultry grit		peat humus or
				sphagnum moss
				or compost

* The soil and humus material that remains above the 1/4- and 1/8-inch mesh sieves

A RICHER DIET FOR PLANTS IN TRAINING

It is common practice to encourage vigorous growth in plants in training by giving them a richer diet than that provided for finished plants. This may be done by at least three methods and innumerable combinations of these methods. One is to add some form of fertilizer to the potting soil when it is compounded; the second is to feed more generously during the growing season; and the third is to increase the proportions of the materials in the potting mixture that contain more nutrients and that stimulate growth.

METHOD ONE: ADDING FERTILIZER

Bonsai, like other plants, require a balanced diet, and whether or not additional fertilizer elements are added to the basic potting soil should depend, to a large extent, on the kind of natural soils used. The main nutrients derived from soil by plants are nitrogen, phosphate, and potash. These parts of a fertilizer mixture are indicated on the bag or container by numbers in that order. In each case, the first number represents nitrogen, the second phosphate, the third potash—the number representing the number of pounds per 100. Many combinations are available, such as 5–10–5, 7–7–7, 6–12–12, etc. The common ones vary in different parts of the country in relationship to the local soil requirements and, to some extent, according to the crop. When all three main elements are included, such formulas are called "complete fertilizers." Plants also require minute amounts of a number of other items in the diet, commonly called "trace elements," but these usually are present in sufficient amounts in natural soils and decaying organic matter.

Strong commercial fertilizers should be used with great caution, because the food elements are quickly available and it is easy for high concentrations in the confines of a pot to produce an unhealthy or fatal condition for the plant.

Some growers use organic fertilizers of much lower food content that slowly become available to the plant over a long period of time, as a result (in part) of the action of decay-producing microorganisms in the soil. A favorite fertilizer used by the Japanese is rape cake, which is the residue after the oil has been pressed from rape seed. A corresponding organic material available in this country is cottonseed meal.

The plant food available in several common organic materials used as fertilizer is shown below. The percentages are rough approximations only, because they vary with the source and treatment of the material:

	Nitrogen	Phosphate	Potash
COTTONSEED MEAL	6	12	1
DRIED MANURE	1 to 2	less than 1	less than 1
BONE MEAL	1 to 3	12	0
BLOOD MEAL	12	1.5	0
UNLEACHED WOOD ASHES	0	1.5	7

If exposed to rain, wood ashes lose much of their potash content. This material also is high in lime and should not be used on acid-loving plants like azaleas and rhododendrons.

If well-rotted, composted barnyard manure is available—a scarce article these days—it may be used safely in fairly large quantities in the potting mixture, and is especially favorable for deciduous flowering and fruiting varieties. Although containing less fertilizer elements by analysis than the dried commercial product, it seems to confer ex-

tra benefits in healthy plant growth. Packaged dry manures usually
have been pulverized and heat-treated to destroy weed seeds. They
are useful organic materials, but cannot be used as generously as the
natural, composted material.

Generally, I do not add fertilizers to my basic potting soil, but occasionally, for plants needing special encouragement, I use a homemade mixture based mainly on organic fertilizers. The analysis is approximately 4–5–5, and it includes dried manure, cottonseed meal,
dried blood, and bone meal. I usually sprinkle some of this mixture
on the rough bottom soil and around the sides of the pot, and then
place a layer of plain soil between it and the roots. The amount:
about a level tablespoon to an eight-inch pot.

METHOD TWO: FEEDING DURING THE GROWING SEASON

Modern soluble complete fertilizers make extra feeding particularly
convenient for plants in training or those requiring a richer diet. There
are a number of brands on the market, some of them dry materials
to be mixed with water, others in concentrated solutions to be diluted.

Watering with a weak solution once a week is the practice of some
growers—others give just two or three feedings per year, in spring,
early summer, and fall. I would suggest using the fertilizer at one
fourth the strength recommended by the manufacturer, or an even
weaker solution. Before going overboard on any feeding program, the
reader is urged to look up further comments on feeding in Chapter 17.

*METHOD THREE: CHANGING THE PROPORTIONS
IN THE POTTING MIXTURE*

Evaluation of the materials usually used in potting soils indicates:

Sand, undecayed sphagnum moss, and such granular mineral material as perlite and granite poultry grit contain no nutrients.

Peat moss, peat humus and leafmold contain small amounts of
plant food, usually in an ascending order as listed here, with very little
in baled peat moss.

Compost may be at about the same level as leafmold, or it can be
about as nourishing as good manure. By "compost" is meant that
rather inexact product of partially decayed organic material, produced
by assembling moist leaves, grass, and other organic wastes from the
garden, which are then allowed a period of three months to a year

for decay. If fertilizer or manures are added when the compost pile is built, the end product can be very rich.

Topsoils used in the loam mixture range from poor to rich. Subsoil clay may contain important mineral elements, but is not considered highly nutritious.

Increased amounts of good loam and compost create a good soil for plants in training. Some growers also consider increased amounts of leafmold helpful, not because it analyzes high in plant food, but because it seems to encourage healthy root growth.

SOME RECOMMENDED VARIATIONS

Pines are drought resistant and grow well in a poor mineral soil. Add one or two extra parts of sand to the basic potting mixture, or the formula could be two parts loam, three parts sand and one part leafmold.

Other needle evergreens are also relatively drought resistant. Add one extra part sand to the basic mixture, or use three parts loam, four sand, one leafmold.

Plants that must produce flowers and fruit are given a richer mixture, with added good topsoil, compost and, perhaps, some organic fertilizer.

Broadleaf evergreens and deciduous plants, some of them of the flowering-fruiting kinds, are generally given a mixture containing additional clay to assure a more constant supply of moisture.

Chapter 12

Potting: The First Transplanting

The first transplanting can be a long step toward converting an ordinary plant to bonsai, or it may be for a period of convalescence after drastic treatment, or merely an important primary stage in a kind of pre-bonsai training. In this chapter are described: (1) the basic potting procedure, (2) the treatment at the first transplanting of plants in differing stages of development, with special attention to certain common problems.

The essentials for potting are: container with an adequate hole, or holes, for drainage; some material, such as window-screen wire, to cover the holes so they will not become clogged; granular material to use in the bottom of the container to assure drainage; potting soil suitable to the plant; tinsnips or an old pair of scissors to cut the screen wire; and a potting stick to firm the soil around the roots. Useful accessories for the operation include: a container for mixing soil, a scoop or trowel for handling this material, a brush for smoothing the top soil and removing dirt from the pot at the conclusion of the operation, and a shallow pan larger than the pot for the first watering. If the display potentials of the plant are important, some kind of Lazy Susan enables pot and plant to be turned easily for observation.

Potting should always be done in a shady place or a work shed shielded from the wind, so roots will not become dry during the operation. Immediately after potting, the plant should be thoroughly watered, and then placed in a protected place out of the sunlight for a period of recuperation.

After selecting a container of the right size and shape, the first step is to cover the drainage openings with screen wire. A common practice in this country is to use curved pieces of broken pots, placed convex side up over the drainage hole, and then some other coarse material, such as gravel, spread immediately above this. This method is satisfactory for bonsai in deep pots. However, for shallow containers, screen wire is more economical of the limited space. Immediately on top of this covering, place a layer of gravel or coarse sand. Some growers then protect this with a thin layer of peat moss, or sphagnum moss, to prevent soil from washing down to clog the spaces below. Next, place a layer of coarse potting soil of a thickness to bring the plant to the right level in the pot.

In potting plants for display, the Japanese rarely locate them in the precise center of the containers. In oblong or oval pots, the plants are placed about one-third distance from one end; in round or square ones, they are placed centrally, but usually, in both cases, slightly back of a center line. In the case of cascade types, the plants are arranged so the over-the-side growth is directly over a supporting foot on the pot, to give maximum stability. The exact placement is governed by the over-all composition of plant and pot.

Once the plant is located in the pot, hold it with one hand; with the other, add soil and then work this into, under, and around the root system. Short jabbing motions with the potting stick are employed to firm the soil in place. As long as the dry, granular soil is lowered by this firming action, more soil is added. As a final step, place a thin layer of fine soil on the surface. At this stage, moss may be used to cover the soil, or dried moss sprinkled on the surface and pressed into place. Now, without delay, water the potted plant thoroughly. An efficient method is to place the pot in a container of water just deep enough to bring the water level slightly below the rim of the pot. At the same time water the top of the plant and the soil in the pot with a gentle spray. Within a few minutes the soil will be saturated.

Plants must be in a stable position in the soil, not subject to excessive movement of the top by wind, if the roots are to make healthy readjustment after transplanting. This often is a special problem with bonsai when relatively tall specimens are planted in shallow containers. To assure stability, sometimes it is necessary to tie or wire the plant in place in the pot until the new roots have gained a firm grip. One way to do this is to pass wires over major roots, at the base of the trunk, and thence down through the drainage holes in the pot where the ends are tied over a nail or stick and tightened. Bits of rubber should be used as padding to prevent damage to the roots where the wire touches them, and the wires should be cut free, after they are no longer required. Another way is to tie stout string around the pot in several places, much in the manner of tying up a package,

Figure 97. To assure stability, sometimes it is necessary to tie a tall plant in place in the pot until the new roots have gained a firm grip.

and then attach strings to these to act as guy lines to steady the trunk.

ADAPT TREATMENT TO THE PLANT

The most dramatic metamorphosis of an ordinary plant to bonsai usually is practical with container-grown and balled-and-burlapped nursery stock that has already achieved good trunk and branch development. If transplanting is done at the most favorable time drastic pruning of both the root system and the top may be undertaken with relative safety. Severe root and top pruning always should go hand in hand.

With container plants, it is normally safe to reduce both parts in the same proportions: if half the top is removed, half the roots may be cut away. Balled-and-burlapped plants, however, already have lost some roots in digging them from the field, so should be treated with more caution. Perhaps a guide would be to say if half or two thirds of the top is removed, one third or a half of the root system may be pruned away. Nursery plants in these two categories can be bought at any time they are available. During periods of the year unfavorable for transplanting, some pruning and training of the tops can be initiated immediately, as described in the next chapter, but repotting, with severe pruning of the roots, should be held in abeyance. Plants in containers may be left undisturbed, as far as the roots are concerned, although in many cases they may need feeding during the growing season before repotting.

Balled-and-burlapped plants are safely handled by putting the undisturbed ball in a box large enough to hold it, and surrounding it with well-drained porous soil. Or, the root balls of such plants can be packed in sawdust or similar material in the same way they are kept in the sales beds of many nurseries. Incidentally, sometimes balled-and-burlapped plants held over in the sales yards from the previous

Sometimes a dramatic metamorphosis is practical with balled-and-burlapped nursery stock that has already achieved good trunk and branch development.

Figure 98. Nursery plant 66 inches.   *Figure 99.* Pruned to 28 inches.

season are excellent buys, if they seem to be healthy and not stunted, because usually they have had time to develop new roots within the ball of soil.

For plants in or approaching the display stage, which are to be put in pots of comparatively small size, the dry, sieved soil mixtures described in the preceding chapter should be used. For plants in training which are to spend a time in large containers or flats, the soil may be the usual porous mixture normally used for florist and nursery stock. In the case of ground beds, sand and some form of humus mixed thoroughly in the upper six inches or so of ordinary garden soil is the right prescription.

SPECIAL PROBLEMS WITH NURSERY PLANTS

Nursery plants grown in this country often present special problems to those who would convert them to bonsai. For instance, many plants today are not grown in soil at all! As soil is such a variable and sometimes unpredictable material, a number of nurseries have turned to the use of soil substitutes of known and constant characteristics. This may be a combination of peat moss and perlite, or ground tree bark and sand, or other mixtures.

Figure 100. In a large container for the first season.

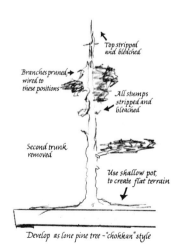

Figure 101. One way this plant might be trained. *James R. Raker*

Soil substitutes are ideal for uniform, fast growth of a nursery crop, where watering and feeding are carefully attuned to the needs of the plant throughout the growing season, but they are far from ideal for bonsai plants in shallow pots. With young, vigorous plants, the better procedure is to wash clean the root system and repot in a more favorable soil. With older, or less healthy plants, however, removal of only part of this soil may be the safe way at first, with a complete change-over spread to two or three repottings.

Another problem noticeable in American nursery-grown plants, from the bonsai growers' standpoint, is the tendency of many roots to grow *upward* from the zone where the rooting starts, the result of a common transplanting practice. In potting rooted cuttings and seedlings that were first started in beds or flats, it is normal for nurserymen to set the small plant rather deep in the pot, with soil firmed around the stem to keep it upright. Roots often grow upward to utilize this soil, as well as round and round the confining area of the pot. The tendency to develop this kind of root structure is then further reinforced by a similar treatment when the potted plant is moved into a larger container or to the field, as again the roots often are pressed deep in the soil to keep the young plant straight.

In some cases, if wayward roots are not too large, and they are not needed, they may be cut off. More often it is better to rearrange the root pattern at the time of the first repotting for bonsai training. One method with older plants is to place a convex rock under the root mass and push the roots downward over it. If the planting is in a pot, wiring, as described in a previous paragraph, can be used to pull the roots downward into the right position. In some cases, rocks placed on top of the roots until they become firmly established in their new positions will serve the same purpose. If the plant is to be grown first in a ground bed, pegs with hooks or padded wire bent into hairpin shapes can be used effectively.

COLLECTED PLANTS

Except in rare instances, or in cases where extensive and prolonged root pruning has been undertaken to prepare the plants for transplanting, the key problem for older plants dug from the garden or the countryside is survival. Therefore, the most favorable conditions for recovery are desired. The move should be made only at the best time for the plant, and the first planting should be in a ground bed or considerably oversize container. Further root disturbance or shortening of the taproot, or extensive training should not be undertaken until a season of healthy growth shows that there has been an adjustment to the first transplanting.

YOUNG PLANTS

Training young plants from the very beginning offers a way to avoid the faults common in older nursery plants, and to develop the plants' habits of growth that are so hard to find. For some tiny *mame* bonsai such training is almost a necessity, as the required compact root system and low branching is rarely, if ever, found growing naturally in certain species.

SEEDLINGS are characterized by a strong taproot and very few side roots at first. A start toward correcting this condition can be made when seedlings have grown large enough to permit transplanting. Common practice is to move them from the container where the seeds have germinated as soon as two or three true leaves have developed, and with care this is safely done anytime during the growing season. The small seedlings are lifted with a flat stick or knife blade, the slender taproot cut back slightly, and then the young plant is either transferred to individual pots or spaced out in a flat. After transplanting, the young plants are kept shaded for a few days. The most effective time to establish a spreading, shallow root system is with one-year-old seedlings. When replanted at this stage, the taproot should be cut back severely and, at the same time, the top growth reduced.

Plants started from CUTTINGS and LAYERINGS do not have taproots, but frequently the rooting proves to be lopsided or unbalanced. As the attachment of these young roots to the stem often is very fragile at first, it is prudent to disturb them very little in the beginning. Either let cuttings remain in the original bed for a season, or replant them with care. After the rootage has become sturdy, the individual roots can be safely rearranged to a balanced pattern supporting the base of the trunk. If there are enough cuttings, it might be well to throw away the badly lopsided ones. To get the roots started off in the right direction, I have found a convenient way is to arrange them over a small cone of soil, or sometimes over a stone chip or pebble placed below them when planting or potting.

It should be noted here that the amount of growth of various roots

Some plants are improved by a season of pre-bonsai training. In this case a grafted flowering apricot is induced to develop an entirely new shallow-root system.

Figure 102. March 4—As it came from the nursery.

Figure 103. A strip of bark is removed just below the point where the bud was inserted in grafting.

Figure 104. Root-stimulating hormone powder applied.

can be influenced somewhat by pruning them, in much the same manner as with branches, described in the next chapter. If a large root is pruned more severely, a smaller one less, the tendency will be for the growth to be somewhat equalized during the following season. However, I have found that severely pruned roots are more liable to die entirely than is usually the case with pruned branches.

It is customary with seedlings, rooted cuttings, and layerings, to use a somewhat more sandy-soil mixture without added fertilizer at the first transplanting. As new growth begins, and afterwards, feeding with weak liquid fertilizer, from time to time, will speed development. After a season of growth, these young plants may be transferred to richer soil for further training.

Figure 105. December 2—After a season in a ground bed, new roots have developed and the old root, below the point where it was girdled, has died. Pruners are used to remove this part.

Figure 106. Now pruned, these healthy roots will be carefully arranged in a balanced position when planted again.

Chapter 13

Training: Pruning and Wiring

Pruning and wiring are the two most effective ways to create, quickly, the proportions of a tree in bonsai. Pruning, for the most part, establishes the proportions; wiring gives emphasis to form and characteristics, helps the composition.

Pruning the top parts of a plant goes hand in hand with root pruning, which means that in most cases, the ideal time for major surgery is just before growth starts in spring, when repotting is undertaken. While there are periods more favorable than others, even fairly heavy pruning can be done at almost any time of the year, with the exception of fall and winter in severely cold climates.

It might be noted that some plants "bleed" sap rather profusely from cuts made at certain times of the year, especially in late winter or early spring. It is possible that this can be damaging, but it is rare. Apparently, gardeners suffer more than the plants. Maple trees have been "bled" for their sugar for a lifetime in New England. Tests at a fruit experiment station have indicated that in a cold climate it is less damaging to grapevines to prune in spring, when they react by bleeding copiously, than in fall, when they do not bleed at all. The objections to fall pruning are that the plant remains pruned and without healing growth for a long time, and sometimes winter injury further "prunes" it. However, sap on the trunks of trees is unsightly. To avoid this, it is common practice with some growers to prune and wire pines, for instance, in the fall and winter.

TOOLS

The tools required for pruning during the training period include sharp garden pruners; a keyhole saw with medium teeth, sharp knife, or razor blade for trimming; and a wood-carving tool for hollowing cuts. Inexpensive wood-carving kits include a handle and a selection of replaceable blades; two or three rounded forms in these blades, in various sizes, are useful. Tree paint may be used for covering exposed wood where larger cuts are made.

OLDER PLANTS

With larger plants that already have good trunk development and that are in the process of being "potted down," drastic changes often are practical. It may be a simple matter to speed up nature's techniques of creating gnarled and bent trunks, and drooping or windswept branches connote age. The objectives in this phase of training are those described in Chapter 9, to create the proportions of a large tree, to suppress or eliminate the juvenile traits.

Reducing the periphery of a plant—the total height and spread of branches—is an effective way of apparently increasing the size of the trunk. Figures 107 and 108 illustrate how trunk size is affected this way, the reduction of the over-all size seeming to make the trunk larger by altering the proportions. Sometimes trees five to nine feet tall are treated this way. The trunk may seem insignificant in the tall tree, but with the same girth in a bonsai eighteen inches high, the reduction of the over-all size creates the illusion of a giant. Of course, in undertaking this kind of alteration plans must be made to avoid any appearance that the top has been chopped off. One way is to train

The illusion of great size in bonsai is created by the proportions. The trunk is the same diameter at "A" in Figure 107 and at "B" in Figure 108. Reducing the periphery and the form of the plant, and altering the proportion of plant to container, effect the change.

Figure 107   Figure 108

a low branch upward, to take the place of the amputated part, to form a new top or leader. Sometimes the cuts can be masked by growth, but in all cases the place and angle of cut should be carefully considered so the telltale marks of pruning will be masked.

Many times the first pruning of a shrub or tree in training as bonsai will follow this order: Most of last year's growth is removed, thus decreasing the periphery. Then branch structure is studied to ascertain the better side to serve as the front of the bonsai. Branches that cross this main view of the trunk are cut off. By reducing the length of the trunk and main branches, sometimes it is practical to increase the taper, from base to tip, of these members. Specifically, this is done by pruning the branch, or trunk, at a point just beyond a selected twig or side branch which thereafter is to be trained as the new terminal growth. Vigorously growing branches without taper are removed entirely. Straight branches are removed, or plans made for training them to a more graceful shape.

Pruning cuts are made either for total removal of a branch, flush with the trunk, or at a point just beyond a side branch—in both cases in a manner to eliminate stubs. Cuts should be smooth, made with a sharp pruner, and saw cuts should be smoothed off with a knife, if necessary. A follow-up treatment for larger cuts is to hollow them out slightly by cutting away some of the exposed wood (not the cambium layer) to speed healing.

Heavy pruning back to old wood is practical for most species, but not for some of the needled evergreens, especially pines. The usual response to pruning the terminal bud, or the end of a branch, is for the dormant buds immediately back of the cut to be activated into growth. Frequently, it is the bud at the last leaf axil behind the cut. Sometimes, two or more buds come to life. Even old branches and trunks of most deciduous and broadleaf evergreen plants will show that there are adventitious buds within the bark that can react to such treatment. Selection of the new growth headed in the right direction, and pruning of other sprouts can direct the desired development.

With pines, and some of the other conifers, adventitious buds do not remain viable in the old branches. For that reason, only part of the new green growth can be safely removed. The usual way to develop branching is to pinch out part of the new growth. With pines, this is a "candle" that first elongates in spring, then becomes clothed with needles. Part or most of this candle of growth can be nipped back. Pines usually respond by forming a number of new buds just below the amputation. This would create a whorl of new branches the next spring, or, sometimes the same season, so normally all but one or two of these buds are removed.

Selection of the point where pruning is done on a twig or branch also can be used to control the direction and shape of branches, without necessarily resorting to wiring. Pick a side bud pointed in the desired direction, then prune just ahead of it. As said before, the bud immediately behind the cut usually makes the most growth. In this manner, by selecting the right buds for new terminal growth, it is possible to guide the development of branches. By repeatedly selecting buds on the same side, the direction can be changed, or a zigzag form can be created by alternately selecting the last bud, first on one side and then on the other. In the case of trees with leaf buds growing in pairs, like maples, control is exercised by cutting out one of these, or by shortening one resulting branch more than the other.

GROWTH CONTROL BY PRUNING

After radical alterations in proportions of the plant have been made in the beginning, pruning of a different kind is used during the first few seasons to control the new growth. Sometimes following severe root and top pruning, a plant goes into a kind of "postsurgical shock," and grows very little the first year. The normal response with the renewal of the root system, however, is for the plant to try to re-establish its stature by producing strong, upright branches characteristic of a young plant. Pruning is the principal means of controlling and directing this. For older plants, often the main need is to develop a twig structure characteristic of a larger tree, accomplished in such cases by repeated nipping of new growth.

Proportions of various parts of plants can be altered through pruning. Unrestrained growth of most plants favors the upper, or more upright branches, at the expense of the lower, or more outward-growing branches. Limiting leaf production of these upper branches, and permitting more leaves on the lower ones can offset this tendency, and will serve to keep both upper and lower parts of the plant in the proportions of healthy growth. This may be done by periodically cutting back new growing points on the upper branches to one or two new leaves, let us say, while, on the other hand, allowing three or four new leaves to remain on the lower branches to be favored. This has a dual effect: of bridling top growth to the pace of the whole plant, and of producing shorter and closer-set twigs and branching in the crown of the tree, which is a characteristic of mature and old specimens.

The rule of tree growth—that the more leaves a branch produces, the more the growth—may be utilized to direct growth as needed. In the case of two branches of equal length, if one is drastically pruned, the other cut back only slightly, the increase in size during the subsequent growing period will be much more for the latter. This is the factor in growth control mentioned above. It also may serve to influence the development of new branches on specimens which have been drastically pruned.

Some species, such as cryptomeria, junipers, false cypresses, etc., grow almost continuously during the season, while others, like pines, may experience only one short period of new growth. There is also a tendency for older plants to grow only during the spring season, while young specimens of the same species may have repeated flushes of new growth—sometimes spring, summer, and fall—if conditions are favorable. It is for this reason that—paradoxically—often it takes less time to make a young plant seem old than to train a plant that actually is old, especially if the latter is in an unhealthily stunted condition. Oddly enough, dwarf varieties sometimes share this same handicap. Naturally dwarfed plants usually are exceedingly slow in developing good trunks. While this is not true in all varieties, it is often the case that the normally fast-growing variety can be dwarfed much more quickly than the natural dwarf.

YOUNG PLANTS

With young, less mature plants, training by pruning may seem a much slower process to create bonsai, but even here it is possible, within a few seasons, to achieve proportions that would require many years for large plants growing naturally.

Guidance by pruning is especially important in growing plants of low stature in those species that cannot be greatly reduced in size because there are few or no living buds in old wood. It is significant in developing small bonsai, those in medium size, and miniature bonsai under seven inches tall. With this objective, especially with conifers, repeated pruning while they are young produces plants that suggest replicas of their elders, with trunk development and branching at a reduced level rarely found among normal seedlings.

To develop the proportions of a real trunk, with thickness and taper, pruning can overcome the infantile slenderness of a seedling. The repeated cutting back of the leading top growth of a seedling can achieve this. Natural dwarfs are occasionally found that are the result of unplanned pruning of a plant, perhaps where roadside mowing repeatedly reduces the top, or where frequent nibbling by livestock limits the stature. Although height is limited in these cases, the trunks slowly become thickened and gnarled. If such naturally dwarfed plants are found, well and good, but usually it is easier to undertake your own dwarfing process.

In the case of young conifers, if the leader is pruned—not back to old wood, but by removing part of the new growth—several buds develop at this point. To develop a main trunk with taper, it is necessary to train one of these to an upright position, usually by wiring, and to cut off the other buds. By repeating this treatment, each time cutting back part of the new leader, a trunk with taper will result.

For most species of deciduous and broadleaf plants, as well as conifers, to the degree practical, development is hastened if pruning during the growing season is not done too quickly. In other words, while in training, plants are allowed to make as much growth as possible, consistent with the branching and form that is planned for them. Thus, a branch may be allowed to grow several inches, perhaps achieve the size of a slender pencil, before cutting it back. The reverse is true in controlling growth of older plants, as explained in a later chapter. The general rule is that the quicker the pruning, the more drastic the dwarfing effect.

Where possible with young plants, it is desirable to allow low branches to grow on the trunk, even though these will later be removed. The reason for this is that the more leaf development occurs above a given point on a trunk, the more increase in girth will result. (See Figure 109.) A few species, such as bald cypress and larch, will develop some taper without lower branches, but most develop very little. Recall the straight, almost up-tapering trunks of pine trees growing in a forest where lower limbs are soon killed by shade. One way to use this influence of a low branch is to permit one at the back of the trunk to remain for a year or more.

WIRING

Of several ways to train branches and trunks, wiring is generally the

Fig. 109. Low branches help develop a tapering trunk.

most flexible and adaptable. Basically, the technique is to wind wire spirally around the member to be trained, and then to bend it into position. After a period of time, the plant will remain in this position when the wire is removed, or rewiring may be necessary.

For older plants being converted to bonsai, the time to wire does *not* necessarily coincide with the first potting and drastic pruning. Although all three of these operations often are performed at one time, for the benefit of viewers at demonstrations, the combination of pruning, repotting, and wiring can prove a shock that sometimes will kill a plant. The safer course is to wait until renewed growth is well started, indicating the re-establishment of a healthy root system.

There is no single ideal time of the year for wiring all species of plants; actually, it is practical to do some wiring at almost any time, if care is exercised to avoid damage to tender buds and leaves, and especially in handling brittle varieties. Perhaps one of the better seasons is in late spring or early summer, when new leaves are fully developed, but before the woody stems have hardened. Bark is more easily bruised at this time, however. I have also found some brittle

Of several ways to train branches and trunks, wiring is generally the most flexible and adaptable.

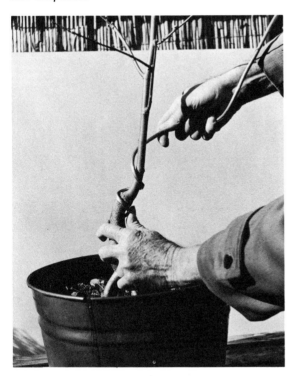

Figure 110. Wire is bent in spiral close to the trunk.

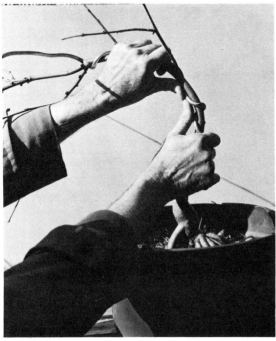

Figure 111. The trunk is gently bent to position.

Figure 112. Feb. 16

Figure 113. June 6

plants somewhat more flexible in late winter, just before buds swell noticeably, but as the sap flow becomes active. The more flexible kinds of plants may be wired in summer, fall, or winter.

It is considered good practice to feed plants a few weeks before they are to be wired. If the work is done in late spring or summer, the plants should be shaded for a few days immediately afterwards.

The ideal branch for wiring is one that has become mature enough to be somewhat woody and firm, so the form will be held when the wire is removed, but not so old that it is excessively hard or brittle, tending to break. Very soft new growth is not suitable for wiring. The ideal-size wire is one just strong enough to hold the member in place.

Wiring is a particularly effective way of carrying out the objectives of training older plants that were begun in large part by pruning. Where branches or the leaders were shortened, wiring is often the means to modify the abrupt change in direction at these points. The periphery of a plant sometimes can be lessened, also, by this means, through giving sinuous or gnarled twistings to the branches. Straight branches can be shaped to an agreeable curve, and side ones can be turned downward in direction. The same downward slant can be achieved by tying with string or other material, but the advantage of wiring is that the curve can be set exactly, and then the end of the branch turned back upward at the tip, in a natural fashion. Branches that tend to obscure the view of the trunk can be moved aside to a more attractive place in the composition. Upright growth of branches in the top of the tree can be made to ramify into a pattern more nearly parallel with the ground.

HOW TO WIRE

To hold a branch or trunk in position, the wire must be large enough to overcome the resistance of the plant, and be anchored at the bottom so it does not turn. The usual procedure in treatment of the trunk is to anchor the wire by inserting one end of it into the soil of the pot, and then to wind the wire at about a forty-five-degree angle upward as far as the training is planned. The wire should be close to the trunk, not a loose spiral, but not gripping it to the extent that it binds. Spacing is a matter that need not be exact, and normally varies from one-half to two inches, depending on the size of trunk and wire, but it should be fairly even. If one wire is not of sufficient strength, a second or even a third can be applied, one at a time, each close to and parallel to the last.

With branches, the end of the wire can be anchored by a twist over itself around the trunk, or if two branches located near each other are to be trained, it often is convenient to use one long wire spiralled out one branch, around the trunk, and then out the other branch.

If there is to be a sideward twist or turn, it is well to spiral the wire over the branch in the direction of the twist, to hold it firmly. When the spiral is in the opposite direction, bending the branch into position will loosen the wire.

AVOIDING DAMAGE

It is easier to avoid the damage that can be caused by wiring than it is to repair it. There are three danger periods worth noting:.

When the wire is first applied, the hazards are in breaking branches, bruising bark or buds, and splitting branches from the trunk. To the beginner I would make the suggestion that you try bending the branch or trunk of another plant of similar kind, age, and size, to see how far bending can be carried without breaking. Experienced growers know which plants are most likely to be damaged and they apply sensitive fingers, much like the storied safecracker, to sense the first almost imperceptible suggestion of breaking, when extreme bending is in order. It should be remembered, also, that it is not necessary to accomplish the planned position in full the first day. Allowing the plant to become almost dry before training, so it becomes somewhat limp as it approaches the wilt point, is also of some help.

New buds and bark of tender species are most susceptible to damage during spring growth, thus earlier or later wiring avoids some of this hazard. It is also prudent to use some kind of padding between the wire and thin-barked varieties. Wire with rubber or plastic insulation is one solution. Or the bark itself can be wrapped in cloth, before applying the wire. Even with species that have particularly tough bark, such as the pines, it is well to use a winding of cloth at a point where an extremely abrupt bend is planned.

To avoid breaking or splitting branches from the trunk, the simple precaution is to hold the branch firmly, usually bracing it with the thumb of one hand, while the other hand carefully bends the branch.

The damage that can be caused by wire during the training period, through girdling branches as they increase in girth, is generally overlooked until sad experience shows the hazard. It may be practical to leave wire, for a year or more, on display plants that have been dwarfed and are making very little new growth, but for plants in training, it is important to make careful and frequent checks, to see that the wire is not binding the enlarging stem. I have found maples

Figure 114. Training wire left in place too long can cause serious injury to the bark, especially in the case of vigorous young trees.

severely wire-cut six weeks after they had been wired in early summer. And, a crape myrtle, seemingly safe in midsummer, had a heavy wire so deeply embedded in the trunk by fall, that it was permanently damaged. The process of growth usually is a fairly rapid elongation of stems and the development of new leaves in spring, and then, it seems, the branches and trunk almost suddenly increase in girth. The moral: Keep a close watch on the wiring of plants in training, and remove any binding wires carefully as soon as noted. Rewire at a slightly different point, if this is needed.

Finally, the third danger period is when the wire is removed. The work of the season can be destroyed in a moment if a branch is broken or torn from the trunk in the process. And this is much more likely than may be suspected, because usually the wire has become stiffer and, at the same time, the branches more brittle, especially if the wire is removed after growth has matured in summer or autumn. The safest way to remove wire, especially the thicker gauges, is to clip it off in short lengths, so a minimum of unwinding is necessary.

Figure 115. The safe way to remove
wire is to clip it off in short lengths.

TOOLS AND MATERIALS

Only one tool is needed in wiring and that is something to cut the wire. The cutting edge of ordinary pliers and angled wire cutters is effective for cutting lengths of wire, in the first place, but those tools are awkward to use, or do not have the leverage for removing wire from the plant. Stout nail cutters of the kind shown in Figure 115 are helpful in this operation. They can be used close to the trunk, without scarring the bark.

Copper wire is preferred for use on bonsai, as this avoids the hazard of rust, which occasionally will kill a branch when iron wire is used.

Solid wire should be selected, rather than stranded or mesh wire of the types used for appliance cords. The latter kinds are too flexible.

A few bonsai specialists offer annealed copper wire in the various gauges most convenient for this work. It may prove difficult to find all size wires that you may want from one local source, but a little shopping around should disclose all the kinds wanted. The most likely places are hardware stores, radio and electronic-supply houses, and mail-order houses. Also, scrap lengths of wire often are available from a local electrical contractor.

Traditionally, the wire used for bonsai training is bare annealed copper. Annealing is done by heating the wire in a fire until it reaches a slightly glowing stage, and then removing it and permitting it to cool naturally. The process renders the wire more flexible, and at the same time removes the shininess of new wire, giving it an attractive brown color. Overheating the wire can cause it to become brittle. If the wire is repeatedly bent in the hands, it will become hard once more, or it will achieve this same degree of hardness as it weathers over a period of time.

Much of the copper wire on the American market already is soft, requiring no annealing. Nor is it necessary to use bare wire, although this kind is less conspicuous. Insulated wire has the advantage of already having a padded covering on it, which minimizes the danger of bruising trunk and branches. The kind of wire pulled through conduits by electricians is in this ready-to-use class, and one listing by mail-order houses, of the type, is called "soft-drawn line wire, neoprene covered." Wire for outdoor use sometimes has a tarred or asphalt-treated waterproof cover, and this should be removed before using it. I have found that burning it off is an easy way both to remove the cover and, at the same time, to anneal the wire.

The most useful sizes of wire are also the ones most commonly used in wiring houses—gauges 10, 12, and 14. Lighter wire is necessary for more slender branches, and this kind is available from stores, in small spools, and as solid bell cord. It is possible to utilize florist wire, which comes in several slender sizes, painted green. Florist wire should not be used for permanent branches, or kept in place very long, if it is used, as it quickly rusts. It is inconspicuous, however, and can control slender branches of tamarisk, willow, etc., which will be removed during or at the end of the season anyway.

For larger trunks and branches, a heavy wire is needed, and one type widely available is called "ground wire," used for grounding house-wiring circuits. This is bare wire, and usually so stiff that it requires annealing. Another wire found in dime stores, in this same heavy-gauge class, is solid-aluminum clothesline. It also can be softened by annealing, but it is difficult to judge visually when it has arrived at the right temperature, and, of course, it remains a bright, unattractive color.

The only other thing needed in wiring is some material, such as strips of cloth, for protecting branches in those spots and cases where it is needed. I have found regular electrician's self-sealing rubber tape very handy, also.

OTHER TRAINING DEVICES

Wiring is not the only method of training bonsai, and often is used in combination with other mechanical means. Soft string is helpful in holding branches in place, sometimes as a first stage in combination with wiring, until the resistance of the plant is less and the hardness of the wire is greater. Sometimes a heavy iron rod is bent to the desired form, and the trunk made to conform to this shape by tying with a soft material at intervals, and with padding to prevent injury.

Splints and braces, also, are of practical use in shaping plants. Contrivances employing clamps or turnbuckles, which can be adjusted from time to time, are helpful in slowly altering older branches or trunks. The possibilities are limited only by the needs of the plant and the ingenuity of the grower.

Chapter 14

Special Kinds of Bonsai

In addition to the methods generally applicable to individual plants trained as bonsai or adapted bonsai, so far emphasized in this book, there are a number of special ways developed by the Japanese for training and displaying plants. These fields are not fully treated here, but certain problems—and opportunities—are commented on briefly as an introduction to a wide range of possibilities the hobbyist may discover for himself in developing interesting individual plants or landscape effects. In some cases, pleasing results can be produced quickly; in others, the training described here involves long-range projects.

Many classifications and styles described by the Japanese are treated in general under the following four headings: Groups and Groves, Bonsai on a Rock, Cascades, and *Mame* or Miniature Bonsai.

GROUPS AND GROVES

There are many classifications for multiple plantings: according to the number of trunks, such as two-trunk, three-trunk, etc.; according to how planted, as individual trees or as a number of trunks growing from a common root; and according to the style of training. What is of special interest to one starting a collection is that within these classes are ways of using plants that do not quite achieve high enough standards to deserve individual planting. Often a tree which has a good trunk, but is too tall or not sufficiently well branched to serve as a specimen, can be combined in a multiple planting. This frequently is done in two-trunk style, where a second tree of somewhat lesser stature helps create an agreeable composition.

Grove plantings, usually of a number of trees grouped off-center in a long, shallow traylike pot, and according to Japanese custom always in odd numbers, offer a way to use young trees effectively. In this case, care is taken to create a natural arrangement with a somewhat taller tree usually serving as the focal point, while indi-

Figure 116. Two trees make an interesting composition.

Figure 117. A grove of trees can be planted, or branches of one tree may be trained as separate trunks although all grow from one root system.

viduals with side branching are placed at the ends, and perhaps ones with lower branching in the background. It is customary to use only one species in such groups, although sometimes two kinds are contrasted. Cluster plantings, that appear like trunks arising from around an old stump, in hexagon or round containers, offer another way of using young trees. Some hobbyists in this country take pleasure in growing seedlings in these two styles, and achieve surprisingly attractive results with some of the trees that have compound leaves, such as *mimosa, pistacia, jacaranda, koelreuteria,* and *melia.* In this case, the compound leaf suggests a branch and individual leaflets the foliage. The varieties mentioned here are tropical or semitropical trees that have the added advantage of growing readily from seed.

Groupings of individual trees in one container sometimes present special problems in training. As they do not necessarily grow at the same rate, they may prove difficult to control. But the short-lived quality of these plantings is offset by the fact that enjoyable results are quickly produced.

Group plantings are not limited to young trees or to a lesser level of bonsai art, however, as there are many outstanding examples that rate among the finest work done by the Japanese.

Among the most impressive of these are groups of trees, each with its separate trunk, but actually all growing from one root. This type is produced by laying the trunk of a tree horizontally on the surface of the soil, or slightly covered, with the root system trained side-wise under it. In the case of needle evergreens, the usual procedure is to select a short specimen with good low branching, remove un-necessary branches, and train the others by staking them to grow more or less upright in the pot. With deciduous trees, often all branches are removed, and the sprouts that come from the trunk, all naturally growing upward, are selected and trained. This kind of training produces a number of notable styles, some of them named (for example) "straight line," "sinuous," or "raft-style." Often the connecting trunk is revealed on the surface of the soil in the pot, at other times it is partially covered.

BONSAI ON A ROCK

Rocks often contribute to the beauty of bonsai. Sometimes they suggest an outcropping near the base of a tree; at other times flat or slightly concave stones are used as containers. Extra care is necessary to maintain plants in such containers, and moss is an important help, both in creating a natural effect and in holding soil around the roots.

The use of stones to be emphasized in this chapter, however, is under circumstances where they are a major element in the landscape effect, and in some cases are predominant.

Low stones can serve as a base to reveal the root structure of a tree. Trident maples, for instance, that develop surface roots readily, may be planted as if they were growing astride an outcropping, "clasp-ing a stone," as one style is called. Proportionately large stones, rising a considerable distance above the soil in the pot, may serve to show an entwining root structure that greatly contributes to the appearance of age.

And finally the extreme of size is reached in tall rocks that suggest by their profile some mountainous crag, planted with small trees and often other plants in a rock-clinging style. Sometimes these large stones are set in soil in shallow trays that are drained in the usual manner. In other cases, they may rest in a low ceramic container or bronze tray that holds water. In containers with soil, the plants usually are trained so their roots reach down into the pots, with roots either revealed on the rock surface, or growing down an inclined surface under moss. When such rocks are placed in basins of water, trees growing on them have their roots confined to pockets of soil on the top or sides. Groves sometimes surmount such a bluff, often a cascading tree clings to the mountainous slope, and many times other small plants are grown in crevices of the rock to create a natural effect. Within the scope of bonsai this kind of planting comes closest to a tray landscape, with a deliberate effort to achieve a natural scene viewed as if from a distance.

Figure 118. A rock may serve to show an entwining root structure that greatly contributes to the appearance of age.

Figure 119. Groves sometimes surmount a rocky bluff to achieve a natural scene viewed as if from a distance.

Before starting any kind of rock planting, certain basic requirements should be noted. For satisfactory results, the first requirement is stability—of the rock in the container, and of the plants on the rocks. Rocks must have a flat base, so they will not tip or move in the container. A suitable stone of good form and texture often is found that does not have a stable base. Some rocks can be chipped or cut to suitable shape. For the hobbyists, however, it may prove easier to brace an unstable base with stone chips. If they are to show, such chips should, of course, harmonize with the main stone, but usually they can be disguised with moss, soil or sand.

There are at least two practical ways of cementing together the materials for such a base. One is with epoxy glue, an adhesive material that comes in two containers which requires equal parts be mixed together thoroughly just before using. This glue is waterproof, requires no tight clamps, and will hold together such dissimilar materials as metal and stone. Another way is to use a nonshrinking type of cement packaged in small quantities in hardware stores. This is sold for use in patching concrete and stonework, and for anchoring iron railings in holes bored in concrete. It tends to hold together stones with rough surfaces, because, unlike ordinary cement, it does not shrink as it dries.

Some hobbyists in this country are using light-weight volcanic or pumice rock which presents no problem in shaping to a flat base. One form of this porous lava foam, called "feather rock," is now widely distributed through building-specialty firms, and because of its lightness—one third or less that of stone—it is favored by landscape architects and others for use in roof gardens and such decorative work as wall facings where additional support has not been provided for regular stonework. Colors range from light gray to charcoal black. Hollows to hold the roots of plants are easily cut in it with a cold chisel and hammer, and it may be roughly formed with such a simple tool as a hatchet. I have found that sharp glasslike particles of the pumice are less likely to fly about if the material is thoroughly wet before work is done on it. The somewhat raw look of the newly quarried lava stone can be mellowed by treating it with a solution of soil containing spores of low-growing mosses, which, in time, will grow to give it a more natural appearance.

Stability of the plant is equally important as stability of the stone. For plants trained over low stones, in cases where the roots actually will encircle the stone and grow beneath it in the pot, all that is necessary is to have temporary ties hold the plant in place for the first season or two. For plants perched on the sides and tops of large rocks, however, the location is too hazardous to depend on the grip of the roots themselves, in most cases. One way to secure the plant is to glue or cement copper wires into the rock in such a way as to tie the base of the tree in place, using, of course, small rubber pads to prevent injury, and covering the attachment with soil or moss. These ties must be checked occasionally and loosened as needed.

For growing over low rocks, any species of plant is suitable that would grow naturally in such a situation. With large rocks, however, the relatively small trees must be chosen from kinds with very small foliage, in order to help create the illusion of a distant scene. Doubtless, for this reason the Japanese favor the very short-needled spruces for this kind of work.

The root structure of candidates for rock plantings is especially important. Plants to be grown in small pockets of soil obviously should have a compact root system. Young plants with strong, long roots are best adapted where they are to clasp the stone, or grown down over a rock, as they are easily trained to grow close to and spread over the stone surface, while old roots are difficult to train.

The Japanese have devised ingenious methods of training roots to meet special needs. With young seedlings, one method is, first, to cut back the taproot; second, the next season, to select the number of roots from the spreading structure that results, and prune the unwanted ones. At this stage, the planting is so arranged that the roots are led downward to good soil, with sand or a poor soil mixture used near the base of the trunk. Roots are thus encouraged to grow longer, and as they do so, they are raised over a period of a few seasons until roots of almost any length can be produced.

In planting trees whose roots are to grow down over rocks, it is the usual practice to first coat the location on the stone surface with a mixture of sticky clay and moss, and then cover the roots with this same material when they are put in place. I have used red clay mixed with sieved sphagnum moss, equal parts by volume of the two, mixed thoroughly. Soft twine or narrow strips of cloth may be used to hold the roots in place, and then a thin layer of moss tied on top of this. Toward the end of the first season, after healthy growth is evident, some of the soil covering the roots may be washed away, by degrees. It is a good idea to plant the rock-and-tree combination somewhat deeper in the soil the first season, in a large container. Some growers start such plantings in a ground bed the first year, entirely covering the rock and roots with soil.

Figures 92 through 96 illustrate the early steps in one rather unconventional rock planting. The plant, a seedling pond cypress (*Taxodium ascendens*), was drastically root-pruned the first year. The second year a new spreading root system developed as it grew in a large, shallow pot, shown in Figure 94. To make it easier to keep soil in place at the base of the heavy rock, a section of hardware cloth was fastened in place with epoxy glue. Roots were arranged around and down the sides of the rock, plastered in place with clay, and tied securely. Moss covered the soil. In this case, it was practical to employ a water-tight container, as pond cypress is one of the few plants that may be grown successfully in a pot without drainage, in water.

CASCADES

The term "cascade" here is used to cover the styles of bonsai which have also been designated by such translated terms as "cliff hanging," "overhanging a cliff," "little, or big fall," or "drooping trunk." Slanting and wind-swept styles sometimes closely resemble these classic forms, but in the former cases the plants do not grow below the rim of the pot, as a rule. In the semicascade class, the branches are lower than the rim, but not lower than the bottom of the pot. In the full-cascade types, the branches descend far downward, thus requiring that such specimens be grown and displayed on high stands.

This form of bonsai should not be confused with cascade chrysanthemums, which are, in fact, grown in a similar, although usually more formal shape, and with emphasis on the masses of flowers. The same varieties of chrysanthemums sometimes are grown in conventional bonsai form.

The prototypes in nature for cascade bonsai are the kinds not uncommon in mountainous regions, where occasionally specimens clinging to a bluff, or the side of a gorge, grow downward in a cascading form. Often there is an upright part in addition to the lowering branches. Apparently, the Japanese see in these trees some of the movement and grace of the cascading streams of their precipitous mountains.

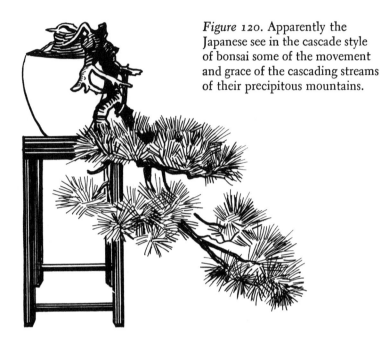

Figure 120. Apparently the Japanese see in the cascade style of bonsai some of the movement and grace of the cascading streams of their precipitous mountains.

Any tree that might be found growing naturally under such conditions is suitable for this kind of treatment, although the ones with less brittle trunks are the more easily trained. Of special note here is that these plants are grown in deep pots, with the base of the trunk usually placed near the edge of the pot from which it cascades, and located directly over a supporting foot on the container.

MAME OR *MINIATURE BONSAI*

The miniature class of bonsai, under seven inches, called by the Japanese *mame* (pronounced mah-may) bonsai, requires somewhat more care and attention than the larger sizes. For the serious connoisseur, the forms and purposes of these small plants is precisely the same as for all bonsai. However, the toylike proportions of plants in this class seem to arouse affection for them in many American growers, and apparently even in some of the Japanese, with the result that often interest is centered, to a greater degree in the plant itself, rather than in the form it represents. Developing *mame* bonsai often becomes a kind of tour de force for the grower, to show what can be done in a container of finger-tip size. A quince four inches tall, bearing a single full-size fruit, probably will arouse, in the viewers, admiration for the skill of the grower, rather than remind them of a tree in nature.

Growing *mame* bonsai of superb quality does, indeed, require great skill, but making a collection of small plants—with less serious intent —is not difficult. And it is fun. Clusters of seedlings might be included, or rooted cuttings with some suggestion of trunk and treelike proportions. Hunting through old pot-bound liners at a nursery may yield interesting specimens. As *mame* bonsai frequently are grown in glazed containers, these small pots add color and interest to a collection.

A more serious approach to *mame* bonsai usually requires attention to special training that starts with young plants, because naturally dwarfed wild or nursery plants of very small size are rarely found. And, even if a suitable plant is located in the countryside, reducing the root system to such limited quarters may not prove practical. Plants for *mame* bonsai, at first, may be grown in somewhat larger pots, or even ground beds, with frequent pruning of top and roots, to develop the required proportions.

Despite the general rule suggested in this book that bonsai culture should not be depended on to reduce the size of leaves, it is possible, with precise care, to grow *mame* bonsai of many species with smaller-than-usual foliage, and—in some cases—the reduction can be dramatic. Elm and zelkova react thus, to some extent, and I have seen small plants of white mulberry, a tree with rather large leaves, growing as *mame* bonsai, with foliage a fraction of the normal size. Some Japanese seem to enjoy growing the parasol tree (*Firmiana simplex*), in part at least, because with skillful bonsai culture plants can be developed with small foliage in a species that is notable for its large palmlike leaves.

There is peril in pursuit of this kind of dwarfing, however. Plants that respond show their ability to withstand unfavorable growing conditions, but the borderline of an unhealthy or fatal condition is close.

The main difference in the culture of *mame* bonsai from the larger sizes is the increased hazard to the plants of the soil drying too quickly. Glazed containers are helpful. More frequent watering, however, is usually required, although ways have been devised by some growers to minimize this. One practice is to keep the small pots sitting on damp gravel in trays on the growing benches, with the water level below the base of the pots, so they will not become water-

Figure 121. Plants in *mame* bonsai proportions have a toylike quality.

Figure 122. A four-inch quince bears a fruit.

Figure 123. A tiny juniper stands 5 1/2 inches tall, planted in a hollow rock that serves as the container.

logged. The water in the gravel adds to the humidity. Other growers sink the pots in damp sand. I have found one way of giving specialized treatment to individual plants is to put each in its own shallow bowl, usually containing some sphagnum moss in the bottom. At the time of daily attention, more water is given to those plants that seem to require it, with the result that some water stays in the bowl for a time, but not so long that it remains overnight.

Feeding also requires more careful adjustment to the needs of plants in so little soil, with frequent feedings of very dilute liquid fertilizer the common practice. And for *mame* bonsai it is customary to repot every year, using a somewhat finer soil than for large plants. If the soil mixture is of the right composition and texture, no drainage material at all need be put over the screened openings in the shallowest containers. For deeper pots, however, some drainage material should be included.

Extra precautions, also, are needed in winter for these small plants. For hardy species to be left outdoors in a deep, cold frame, I have followed the practice of sinking the containers in larger pots, or flats, containing a mixture of sand and peat moss. And sometimes I have removed the plants from their pots—easily done, because the matted roots hold the soil tightly together by the end of the growing season —and sink the root balls in the peat-sand mixture. In some places growers keep the *mame*-size plants in a special glass-enclosed area of a cool greenhouse, where moisture and humidity can be controlled more easily. The danger is that during the season when these small plants do not need daily attention, the occasional watering which they do require may be overlooked.

Chapter 15

Variations in Treatment and Response

No set of simplified rules of training and care is applicable to all the kinds of plants which can be grown as bonsai or adapted bonsai; species vary in their habits of growth and in their needs, with the result that both the objectives sought for a plant and the practical methods used also must vary. The problem of describing methods is that if they are really simplified and concise, the picture created tends to become untrue, because the many exceptions are not included. If all the exceptions to the rules are noted as we go along, the result is a lengthy description of qualifications so ponderous that it becomes confusing. Other chapters in this book describe bonsai methods in general. This chapter includes descriptions of some of the variations in training methods and responses, illustrated by specific plants.

This is not a list of the better varieties for bonsai. The plants mentioned here were chosen merely to indicate the wide variation in treatment, and my only criterion was that they were among the plants with which I have had personal experience. Some are kinds not particularly suited to bonsai, although they can be given a bonsai style of training.

In this short list there are flowering species that bloom only on new terminal buds, and those that blossom on the older stems and trunk; varieties that are easy or difficult to transplant, wire, or prune; some that require a hearty diet and lots of water; others that are better grown in a drier sandy soil; plants that benefit from repotting more than once in one year; and plants that should be repotted infrequently.

I am sure that the suggestions on cultural methods offered here are not the only ways these plants can be well grown; they are simply descriptive of the kind of treatment I have found reasonably successful under my conditions.

MAPLES (*Acer*), especially the small-leaf and cut-leaf forms of the

Japanese maple (A. *palmatum* and varieties of *dissectum*), trident maple (A. *buergerianum*), and Amur maple (A. *ginnala*). These are small trees, with many good characteristics for bonsai. Foliage in spring is delicate and often colorful. Some forms are red and remain so throughout the summer, and most kinds turn to beautiful autumn shades.

Maples in general are subject to leaf scorch, a condition in which the ends of the leaves turn brown and curl, as if burned. In extreme cases, all the leaves turn brown and fall, even though the plant is not, necessarily, killed. The condition is caused by dry air and hot summer sunshine.

Young Japanese maples tend to grow rapidly in spring, with long internodes. It is a good idea to give them as much sun as possible in this early period of growth, and then put them in some shade during very hot weather. After four or five leaf nodes have developed, cut back to one or two nodes. Repeated pruning to one or two nodes helps control form and develop branching. Leaves and branches come in pairs, from the opposite sides of the branch. The usual practice is to remove one of these buds, or to shorten one of the resultant branches more than the other. Leaf pruning is a technique applied in particular to maples. In early summer, in the case of vigorous plants, all leaves are removed with scissors. With old plants sometimes alternate leaves or part of the leaves are trimmed. This is said to result in finer autumn coloration, but it has not proved a major factor in my climate where color usually is good anyway. Autumn colors result from a rather exacting set of weather conditions, and it is not a sure bounty for bonsai maples in all areas, but a very beautiful quality if present. Leaf pruning does result in second-growth leaves that are smaller, more deeply indented, and of more delicate appearance. It also often induces another period of branching growth, which is useful in training young plants. Old or weak plants should be fed a month or so before leaf pruning. (Note of warning: Total defoliation is never carried out with needled evergreens, and rarely with broadleaf evergreens.)

Stems and trunks of maples are brittle and must be wired and bent with great caution. A slow, step-by-step change of position for a branch or trunk is advisable. Branches and trunks of fast-growing maples in training are scarred quickly by tight wire, sometimes in a matter of weeks in early summer. Check wires frequently, remove and replace as often as necessary to avoid damage. Repotting may be done annually, or every two or three years, according to how much the growth of the plant is to be hastened.

AZALEAS (*Rhododendron* according to botanical classification, but commonly listed as azalea in the trade. Varieties have been cultivated for so long that their heritage is not certain). The dwarf evergreen kinds, such as the Kurumes and the Satsukis, with small foliage, are particularly adaptable. In colder climates certain varieties (Hinodegiri and Coral Bells, among the Kurumes, for instance) often have beautiful autumn coloration that remains most of the winter. Usually, in late winter or early spring, blooms cover the foliage in solid masses. In mild climates where there is no pronounced period of dormancy, some azaleas may bloom intermittently much of the year.

Characteristically shallow root systems make culture of azaleas in pots of moderate depth rather easy, and in general they will bloom well each year when grown in considerably more shade than most flowering plants. Flowers, however, are not the only—nor even the most important—characteristic: some old Satsuki azaleas with massive, gnarled exposed roots are among the most handsome and expensive bonsai available in this country today.

Old trunks and even fairly small older branches are very brittle. In fact, altering their position very much is so hazardous that pruning is a major way of training old specimens. Where a good trunk or old root system is discovered, drastic stubbing-back of branches is a practical method, because these plants sprout readily with many new buds coming to life in old wood. New growth a year old is relatively simple to train with wire. Branches are split easily from the trunk, and the bark may be bruised badly, especially in spring. Wrap the trunk with cloth, or use insulated wire. I have discovered that bending and wiring is a little easier to do in early fall, after allowing the plants to become almost wilted by keeping them drier than usual. Spring wiring, however, has the advantage of being removable by the following winter, thus eliminating the wire from the plants when they are in bloom.

The most favorable time to repot is immediately after the blossoms begin to fall, or in mild climates, during a comparatively dormant period. To train and to maintain shape new growth starting immediately after the blooming season should be trimmed at once; if pruning is continued after the early summer period, flower buds for the next spring will be removed. Not much feeding should be necessary, nor is it desirable, if a fairly humusy-soil mixture is used. I rely mainly on peat moss, plus some sand and granular clay. An exposure with half shade is indicated for azaleas, and even more shade in very sunny climates. Soil should not be permitted to become too dry between waterings.

For massive bloom, most azaleas require a cool period for the blooming wood to mature buds properly. In our climate, allowing plants to remain outdoors for the first frosts and cold weather in fall is satisfactory. After that, I bring plants into a cool greenhouse, keep them well watered, and move them to a slightly warmer location as buds begin to fatten. Buds and blossoms remain effective for many weeks, if the plants are kept out of direct sun and in a cool place. If repotting seems indicated, it should be done as the flowers fade and at the same time that some pruning is undertaken. Plants are kept cool but protected indoors, in good light, until the danger of hard frost is over.

FLOWERING QUINCE (*Chaenomeles*) Dwarf forms, of *C. japonica maulei* in particular, are handled easily. Old plants usually survive, if both top and roots are severely pruned at the start of training, but it takes some time for such a specimen to develop a new branch structure to overcome the pruned look. With flowering quince this branching is important, because one of the most attractive periods occurs when this species blooms in winter or early spring before leaves unfurl. Wiring is done easily at any time. Exuberant new growth in spring should be cut back to one or two nodes. Many kinds of quince develop flower buds on old wood, so pruning may be carried on as late in the season as desired. Repot in fall or early spring.

If potted plants are brought indoors in midwinter, are kept well watered in a cool place, they soon will bloom. Flowers of deep hues are much lighter when grown indoors out of sunlight, and are especially beautiful. There are varieties that bloom at other seasons, and some will set fruit. In cold climates, give the same kind of protection as for azaleas until the worst of the winter weather is over, then gradually accustom them to the outdoors. Give plants full sun in spring, part shade in summer.

HOLLY (*Ilex*) Several hollies with small leaves are good material for bonsai. Two of them are outstanding. One of these greatly favored by the Japanese is the Siebold holly, *Ilex serrata*, a deciduous holly with small, finely serrated leaves. Bare branches of female trees, that have had proper pollination of blooms in spring, carry bright-red berries late into winter on the bare branches—if birds do not eat them. This species develops handsome trunks with gray bark, and with pruning can develop a compact branching habit. Repot early each spring, with considerable pruning of the growth of the previous year. To permit flower buds to develop, growth should not be trimmed too much until buds set. Branches then can be shortened safely as needed. Branches break easily. Wrap or use insulated wire to play safe, although with extra care, soft copper may be used. Plants thrive and fruit better with maximum sunlight and frequent watering. *Ilex decidua*, a native American holly, is similar, and is being used by some growers in this country.

A Siebold holly at the start of training is shown in Figures 124, 125, 126, and 127. The twisted trunk of this plant had been broken in the nursery. The first year, in a training pot, the plant was encouraged to grow vigorously, to develop branches which, in time, would be trained to create better taper and transition from the thick trunk to the twiggy branches. This plant-in-training also serves to illustrate root pruning and repotting, in Chapter 17.

The second especially good holly for creating interesting bonsai is the Japanese holly, *Ilex crenata*, and in particular, the dwarf forms, such as *Helleri*. This is an evergreen holly with very small leaves that bear no resemblance to the spiny kinds used for Christmas decoration. The leaves are finely serrated and oval. The female trees bear black berries. Rooted cuttings of the dwarf varieties, in one or two seasons, will grow into compact specimens of low stature. If care is taken to arrange the root systems carefully at the first transplanting, it is a simple matter to take advantage of the tendency of this species to form massive roots near the surface. Within a few seasons, very effective specimens can be trained. Repot in early spring. Trim in spring and at any time to control and to direct growth. With care, wiring is not hazardous and can be done at any season, if the plant is vigorous. Give sun and water frequently.

JUNIPERS (*Juniperus*; several species and forms). There are so many junipers, including some trees commonly called cedars, that it would seem impractical to generalize about them. As a family of needled evergreens, however, they stand in rather sharp contrast to pines, described also in this chapter. Both pines and junipers are

Stages in training a Siebold Holly (Ilex serrata)

Figure 124. March 4—Plant in training pot.

Figure 125. April 15—Repotted and after growth has started.

Figure 126. June 18—In full leaf, growth more upright.

Figure 127. Training of branches begun by tying them with string.

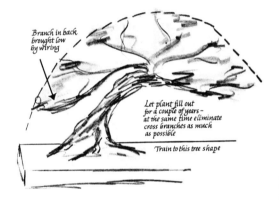

Branch in back
brought low
by wiring

Let plant fill out
for a couple of years –
at the same time eliminate
cross branches as much
as possible

Train to this tree shape

Figure 128. Sketch suggests further objective.   JAMES R. RAKER

favored highly for bonsai culture. The junipers, as a general rule, are much more easily transplanted, even as older wild specimens. Growth is almost continuous during spring and summer, requiring a constant nipping of new foliage. Junipers, varieties with which I have had experience, usually will sprout with fair reliability from older wood. They are particularly tenacious of life, surviving adversity and mistreatment. Parts of a plant may continue in good health, while other parts are killed, the bark withering and the wood becoming whitened with the passage of time. For this reason, junipers are particularly effective when used in the driftwood style of bonsai, with the bleached wood of the dead parts contrasting dramatically with the healthy green of the remaining branches and live bark.

As trunks of moderate size are fairly pliable, branches have sturdy attachment to the trunks, and the bark is not easily damaged, there is not much danger in training plants by wiring and bending.

There are many native species of junipers in various parts of the country that have been collected successfully, as well as the ornamental forms that are widely available from nurseries. The small foliage type of *Juniperus chinensis Sargentii*, called by the Japanese "Shimpaku," is not widely grown in this country, but there are other

Fifteen-minute change from nursery plant to adapted bonsai.

Figure 129. Nursery-grown juniper (*J. procumbens*) in original pot.

Figure 130. Partially pruned and in a cascade bonsai container.

Figure 131. Wire applied to change position of branches.

Figure 132. Initial wiring and pruning complete.

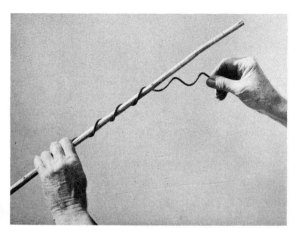

Figure 133. How insulated wire was preformed by twisting it around a stick the same size as the branch. This is not common practice in applying training wires to bonsai, but is conveniently used for plants of this character.

cultivated forms that become good bonsai, if properly trained. Smooth, compact balls of foliage especially are favored with some junipers; this is the result of careful—and almost constant—pruning throughout the growing season. Some hobbyists here start training by shearing the foliage with scissors, to get the basic shape quickly, and then later use tweezers, to remove the brownish tips that result from cutting in this way. But the standard way to prune is to pull out the new growing tips with the fingers, **being** careful not to damage tender foliage nearby.

Repot every two or three years, using a standard potting soil with a little extra sand.

LANTANA (*Lantana Camara*) This is not a plant for bonsai in the traditional Japanese manner, but it is well known to American gardeners for its habit of almost continuous bloom when used in beds or window boxes. It is a tender shrub that is killed by hard frost, so it is commonly handled as a bedding plant started from new plants each spring. Some gardeners here have trained lantanas as standards, or treelike forms, three to five feet tall. These may be moved to the garden in summer, or kept all year in a large tub. If such plants can be stored safely from frost in winter, they may possibly outlive their owners. The usual way to develop standards is to train a young lantana plant upward on a stake the first year, keeping side branches pruned to some degree. When the desired height has been achieved, the side branches are removed, and the branching at the top nipped a few times, to produce further branching in a treelike top structure. By rubbing off any new sprouts on the trunk, and periodically hard pruning the top branches, these standards are kept to the required form from year to year.

One Japanese bonsai technique—of repotting certain vigorous plants in the middle of the growing season—has particular application to lantanas grown in containers. The Japanese treat willows, tamarisks, crape myrtles, and some other plants with this midseason repotting, which seems to be a denial of the general rule to repot only when plants are dormant. Because all flowers on lantanas are produced on buds of the current season, hard pruning at any time is practical. Therefore, for midseason repotting, the plant is simply pruned of two thirds or all of its current growth, repotted in fresh soil, watered thoroughly, and put in the shade for two or three days. Back in a more sunny place, the plant quickly sprouts new branches. When these are a few inches long, nip out the terminal buds to produce more branching. Soon thereafter, the plant will be clothed in new, healthy foliage, with a new crop of blossoms. This is a practical way to overcome the tendency gardeners here have observed in these plants, of losing good foliage color, slowing down in bloom, and requiring more than once-a-day watering towards the latter part of summer. In climate zones with a long summer this repotting may be done twice during the season, and plants can be brought indoors to continue in bloom. Where winter sunlight is weak and the air indoors is dry, lantanas are not particularly good houseplants, however. To conserve space, I prune the plants hard just before frost, and store them where there is some light and where the temperature is cool but not freezing. They are watered just enough to keep them from becoming dry during winter. In early spring, the plants are repotted and taken outdoors after danger of frost is past.

For training in a bonsai manner, young plants at the first repotting should have their roots arranged carefully, to avoid the round-and-round pattern common with florist potted plants. Then the training for standards is carried out as usual, except that to achieve much taper in the trunk it will be necessary to allow some low branches to grow, perhaps for several seasons, removing the older ones from time to time, and allowing new ones to develop. Lantana is a plant perhaps better used as a moderately large terrace plant, and it is most easily trained to an umbrella-shaped mass of foliage and flowers that mask the stubby main branches which have been repeatedly pruned. Plants should be fed and watered generously, and put in a position where there is considerable sunlight. I have used extra amounts of granular clay in the potting soil, to try to meet the heavy demand for moisture. Flowers that decorate these plants are borne in small nosegays, in some varieties all white or yellow, or pinkish lilac, but in many cases the colors are a mixture of yellow to orange at first opening, then change slowly to pink and rose as the blossom ages.

MALPIGHIA (*Malpighia coccigera*) This genetic group of tropical American plants called Malpighia is so little known to gardeners here that probably there is no useful common name. The species of interest is *M. coccigera*, a dwarf evergreen West Indian shrub sometimes grown in south Florida as a hedge or ornamental. I have heard it called box holly or holly box, but I doubt that these terms will be helpful in finding it. Some Far South nurseries carry it, and it is available from specialists in greenhouse tropical plants in other parts of the country. There is only one other Malpighia of special renown, and that is the Barbados cherry (M. *glabra*), made famous by the discovery that its fruit is extraordinarily rich in vitamin C.

The dwarf *Malpighia coccigera* for bonsai has tiny, very glossy leaves, some of them smooth ovals, others on the same branch with hollylike spines. Flowers are pale pink, about a half inch across, with a crepelike texture. Plants soon develop trunks and interesting surface roots. Their proportions recommend them for *mame* and small bonsai. Developing branches requires constant nipping, and this pruning does not interfere with blossoming, as the flower buds develop on old wood, occasionally even bursting from the bark on the trunk.

The period when the plant is most attractive is when it is covered with pink, oval buds—just before the flowers open. Plants have bloomed two or three times a year for me. Malpighia is killed by frost, so must be brought indoors, or into a greenhouse in winter, in most areas. It is also sensitive to drought, and will die if allowed to become too dry.

PINES (*Pinus*; many species and varieties). These take first place in Japanese gardens and as trained miniatures with many bonsaimen. Pines rate other near superlatives. They are among species less likely to survive importation treatment, although some importers have had notable success. Old specimens must be handled with great care, however, and it is very difficult to find Japanese-trained plants here, and almost impossible to locate the leaf and bark forms of Japanese white, black, and red pines (*Pinus parviflora, Thunbergii* and *densaiflora*) most favored in Japan. Fortunately, there are native American species which have proved good counterparts to the ones in Japan, but—again—transplanting naturally dwarfed old specimens from the wild, ranks among the most difficult transplanting operations. Some of the short-leaf pines native to this country are listed in Chapter 5.

Nursery-grown pines are not so hard to handle, and, once established in containers, are particularly satisfactory. They thrive on adversity, are resistant to drought, and actually produce more tidy growth on what seems to be a starvation diet. These enduring qualities might be guessed by the fact that pines, in some parts of the United States, are nominated as most likely to succeed on poor mineral soils and rocky slopes, when planted as one-year seedlings.

In bonsai culture, it is customary to pot pines in a very sandy soil mixture, sometimes simply river sand and some leafmold. I have seen nursery plants in containers of peat moss and sand still growing sturdily after several years of neglect. Even pines in training should not be given an overrich soil mixture.

Pines are easily trained by wiring and bending, as even fairly old trunks and branches are relatively supple in all seasons, and the bark is not easily damaged. Protective wrapping is required only at points of drastic bending. Pines generally resist training, however, and tend to unbend when the wire is removed. This means that, in many cases, rewiring must be done for several years. Many growers wire pines in fall or winter, in part to get the task out of the way before the rush of spring work with other varieties, but mainly to avoid the flow of whitish resinous sap that sometimes is an unattractive by-product of little nicks or minor damage done to the bark, if training is carried out in spring or summer.

Pines cannot be cut back drastically, because adventitious buds do not remain viable for long in old wood. The few species of pine that do sprout from old wood do so unpredictably and are not necessarily long lived. Pruning, therefore, is limited to shortening new growth, always leaving some needles on green wood, behind the cut. Pruning to train and limit growth, usually performed just once a year, is explained in more detail in the next chapter.

Basic requirements for pines are good drainage, sunshine, and a location with good air movement. Repotting is required only every three to five years, and old plants in large containers are repotted even less frequently. Feeding is rarely given during the active growing season in spring. Feeding practice, as in all cases, is modified somewhat by the kind and quantity of soil in the container, but usually just one or two feedings, in summer and fall, are considered enough. Pines vary widely in their hardiness, but in general native species in their own areas can be left outdoors with little or no protection, except in places with very severe winters.

BALD AND POND CYPRESS (*Taxodium distichum* and *ascendens*) Many unrelated trees are called cypress, but the ones meant here are the species that thrive in swamps in the South. These beautiful trees are not commonly grown as ornamentals, the neglect probably stemming from the fact that it is not generally known they will grow very well on dry ground as well as in swamps. Too, they are hardy farther north than their southern habitat would suggest. Tourists, impressed by the

massive buttressed trunks of these trees, and the root "knees" rising
above the water in swampy places, plus the festooning moss on their
limbs, are apt to overlook their delicate foliage. This has particular
charm. In summer, it is light green; in autumn it often turns a rust
or rose-brown. Sometimes there are two-tone effects, with lower or
inner branches having leaves more nearly yellow and upper ones—
red-brown. Foliage of both species is similar on young trees. In youth
and in later years, the swamp cypress (*T. distichum*) bears what appears to be small, compound, flattened leaves, but these in fact are
twigs bearing small, true leaves. Upward-growing and elongating twigs
usually remain on the tree in autumn, but the lesser ones fall, twig
and all. Some Japanese bonsaimen call our native tree "feather-falling
pine," an apt descriptive term.

In the case of pond cypress (*T. ascendens*), as the tree grows older,
the twiglets grow upward (ascend) from the branches, and the leaves
no longer open outward but remain small and awl-like, closely gripping the twig. The foliage of pond cypress is somewhat similar in detail to that of the giant sequoia, and bald cypress leaves look like
those of the Coast redwood. Bald cypress leaves are almost identical
with those of dawn redwood (*Metasequoia*), but are superior for bonsai because they are much smaller. Dawn redwood now is distributed
widely by nurserymen, mainly because of the romantic story of its
being a rediscovered "prehistoric" tree. All these species are closely
related.

These southern cypresses usually develop good tapering trunks,
without the necessity of leaving low branches at the first part of training. In my experience, they may be pruned drastically to any degree
desired, and will usually respond by promptly developing new
branches from many points on the trunk. Mature branches are easy
to bend, and the bark is tough and resistant to damage. Unlike pines,
cypresses quickly accept the trained position, and usually hold it when
the wire is removed, even after a few months.

These taxodiums are among the few bonsai plants that can be
grown safely with their roots in water, without drainage. Pots may be
placed in trays of water in summer, thus simplifying care for display
plants and encouraging plants in training to make continuous growth.
Ordinary watering is all that is necessary for health, however. To develop branch and twig structure, constant nipping with the fingers
of the tips of leafy twiglets and branches is required. Pruning can be
done at any point with the expectation of new growth immediately

back of the cut. In cold climates, plants in containers should be protected against hard freezing, perhaps in a deep cold frame or cool greenhouse.

WISTERIA AND CRAPE MYRTLE (*Wistaria*; several species and *Lagerstroemia indica*). These are two plants of many differences and a few similarities when grown as bonsai.

Wisteria (the spelling changes thus in common usage), a cold-hardy, vigorous vine with large foliage, hardly seems a candidate for bonsai, but it has characteristics that lend themselves to effective use for at least certain periods of the year. A few long flower clusters suspended from bare branches of a bonsai-trained wisteria, in spring, are, of course, breath taking—almost too beautiful and oriental to meet the standards of a connoisseur. For those who would like to create a very old bonsai in a very short time, however, wisteria has another trait that can be exploited: If the top is pruned drastically, even large and old trunks can be transplanted. In midwinter I have dug from the garden a wisteria with a knotty base of a trunk 19 1/2 inches in circumference. At the first move, into a rather large tub, all top growth was removed and the trunk shortened to a few inches; large roots, one of them 1 3/4 inches in diameter, were reduced to three-inch stubs or less. Late in spring, the plant leafed out, and quickly became re-established the first summer. The next year, it was repotted in a large bonsai container, and training of the branches begun.

This ability to survive transplanting, if the top is pruned severely, is not unique with wisteria; in fact, it is the trade secret of many growers, making conversion to bonsai practical for old plants of many species. Another example is crape myrtle, a well-known summer-flowering shrub in the South. Crape myrtle is thought to be difficult and unpredictable in transplanting, even by some nurserymen in the warmer parts of this country, where crape myrtle is widely grown. The difficulty lies in the reluctance of home gardeners to prune the top of plants they buy. If the top is cut far back, huge crape myrtle can be moved easily. For American gardeners who have learned that generally more care must be taken in transplanting large plants, the easy results can be astonishing. Since summer bloom is a particular feature of crape myrtle, it is practical to mask the amputated trunk with foliage at that season, until a new branch structure has been trained. Flower buds are formed in the terminal buds of new growth, so summer pruning must be timed carefully not to eliminate the flowers. One practice is to shorten new vigorous branches just once in late spring, and then allow growth to develop unhindered.

On the other hand, wisterias need an attractive branch structure if they are to be effective when they are almost bare of foliage in early spring. And, in the cases of the wisterias with which I have had most experience, the spring flowers seem to develop from the growth of the previous year, or the year before that. This indicates an entirely different pruning technique, if flowers are to be featured. In spring, the plants attempt to regain their vining habit by making new growth at an amazing rate. These long, willowy branches should be shortened to four or five leaf nodes, and recurrent growth later should be cut back to one or two buds. Wisteria is an unpredictable bloomer, which in the garden usually waits until the vining branches have overgrown the top of their support and are in full sun. Pruning practices alone will not produce flowers on wisteria bonsai. A sunny location, ample feeding, and generous watering seem to be the requirements for both wisteria and crape myrtle. The need of wisteria for water is so great that some growers set the pots in trays of water in summer. Extra amounts of clay are also usefully incorporated in the potting soil for both these plants.

Crape myrtle and wisteria react differently to wiring. Wisteria branches, at first, are too limber to train by wiring, then rather quickly seem almost too brittle. The bark is split easily from the older stems, if much bending is done, and this hazard is signaled by a crackling sound as the branch is bent, the bark splitting lengthwise. If not carried too far, no great harm is, necessarily, done; I have bound such places with rubber tape, and they soon healed. Slow bending, over a period of time, seems to be the better way. Girdling by wire is not a serious hazard. Wisteria is hardy in most of the country, and requires very little winter protection.

Crape myrtle branches and trunk are fairly easy to bend, and although care should be taken not to damage it, the bark is resistant to injury while wiring. The great danger is in the wire biting into the branches and trunks as they increase in girth in summer and fall. Protection by wrapping, or by the use of insulated wire, is not enough to prevent damage; a close watch must be maintained, and the wire loosened or replaced as needed. Crape myrtle is not hardy in the North, and must be protected from hard freezing. Light frosts in the fall months do it no harm, however, and the foliage at that time often turns to autumn hues.

PART IV

CARE A SIMPLE ROUTINE

Chapter 16

Keeping Them Small—and Healthy

No single aspect of bonsai culture mystifies the uninitiated more than the one that elicits the oft-repeated question "What keeps them small?" Experts and amateurs alike in the field of Western horticulture have been theorizing on this Japanese "secret" for almost a century. Some of these opinions have been based on sound observation of plant growth habits. But usually the theorists, no matter how competent in other fields, have had no actual experience in growing bonsai. The factors they have pointed out range from the effects of inhibiting growth by twisting and bending down branches, planting in very poor soil in small pots, limiting food and water to the extent that the plant is reduced in health to a point closely approaching death, and finally to the most widespread current notion that it is mainly due to root pruning. All of these measures can be part of bonsai culture, and some of them, it has been noted already, are of considerable hazard to the life of the plant.

Basic to the purpose of bonsai culture, however, is keeping plants healthy, as well as small, and many factors—some of them mentioned in other chapters—are of importance. But by far the most significant of the factors which keep plants in bonsai proportions is pruning.

A rather common notion is that pruning invigorates a plant, and indeed vigorous new growth is observed when healthy plants are pruned *occasionally*. This is the way fruit trees react to infrequent or once-a-year pruning. Hard pruning does renew such plants as rose bushes, which are fed generously so they will produce new wood for flowers. But pruning, aside from the removal of deadwood, is, in fact, a dwarfing process if continued over a period of time, with the amount of the dwarfing being directly proportional to the amount and frequency of pruning. This is explained simply enough by a reversal of wording of one of the basic rules of plant growth—"the fewer leaves, the less growth."

The kind of pruning that controls the size of bonsai limits the amount of new growth each year; it may be a once-a-year treatment for some species, or it may be applied repeatedly, according to the growth habits. Rather than stunting a plant, in the common usage of the word, this pruning helps it to continue in good health. Although the prime objective is to control size and form, such pruning holds in check unlimited top growth, which in most cases, would result in root growth that would overfill the container. In the latter event, the plant would become stunted.

There is a partnership of roots and leaves spelling mutual interdependence. It is obvious that where roots are limited to a small pocket of soil—as they are sometimes found in nature—eventually there is a limiting of stunted top growth. Less obvious is the fact that when top growth is limited by repeated pruning there is a limited amount of root growth. If one were repeatedly to prune all new growth from a plant, immediately as it started, the development of roots would be limited severely, and soon would stop.

Top growth and root growth are related, although they are not always in unison. Roots of many plants will grow in fall, even at times when the tops show no evidence of activity. Root growth also may start first in spring, although in many cases the above-ground portion of the plant calls on stored reserves, to initiate growth before roots become active in cold soil. The significance of this relationship of growth below and above ground in bonsai, no matter the timing, is that the limitation in one of these zones creates limits in the other.

EFFECT OF ROOT PRUNING

The reaction to root pruning perhaps is better considered here as an influence on growth, rather than in the following chapter which describes the actual operation of repotting and root pruning. In some cases, at the beginning of training, when a plant is severely root-pruned it may react to the shock by growing very little the first year. But this response is exceptional. After repotting, the reaction to moderate root pruning of a healthy plant of balanced top and bottom development usually is a flush of invigorated top growth, often to an extent that surprises and embarrasses one who had thought root pruning was the key to keeping a plant small. The reaction, however, is logical; remove some old roots, provide fresh soil for new roots—*ergo* —new buds and leaves above ground, as well as new growth below. The most important purpose of root pruning in bonsai is to make it possible to keep a plant healthy in a small container, by providing fresh soil and room for new roots to grow.

ALL PLANTS MUST GROW

How bonsai proportions are developed and maintained will differ with the species, with the purpose of the grower and, to some extent, with the age of the plant. All plants, however, must make new growth each year to remain healthy. Broadly speaking, there are two classes of plants, as far as pruning is concerned: (1) Those which are permitted to become larger very slowly, by severely limiting new growth. (2) Those which are maintained, more or less, at the same size, from year to year, by renewal pruning that removes all or different parts of new growth periodically.

Figure 134. Increase in size is limited to an amazingly slow rate in the case of such bonsai as pines. This Japanese white pine (*P. parviflora*) is 23 inches tall and about 40 years old.

In the first class by necessity are those plants, mainly among the conifers, which do not produce new buds on old wood, or respond unpredictably and slowly to hard pruning. The pines are prime examples. The increase in size of such plants can be held to an amazingly slow rate, as shown by the photographically documented specimen in Figures 136, 137, 138, and 139. This pine is one of a collection given by Ernest F. Coe, of New Haven, Conn., to the Brooklyn Botanic Garden in 1925. It was uprooted originally from a mountainside in

Figure 135. A kind of renewal pruning makes it possible to keep many species, such as this 25-inch Chinese hackberry (*Celtis orientalis*) in almost static proportions.

Japan, trained by the Japanese as bonsai, and later imported by Mr. Coe. Had this tree grown unrestrained in open ground, doubtless it would be at this age a forest giant.

Specifically for pines, growth develops and is limited in this manner: Each spring a bud (or buds) at the end of each twig elongates in the form of an upright candle. In due time, bundles of needles develop from the sides and end, to form the new crop of foliage on this extension. In order to prune, the candle is shortened as the needles develop, the amount depending on the degree of restraint desired. Candles on young trees or branches, to be permitted greater growth, are not pruned as severely. For older trees two or three bundles of new needles are usually considered a minimum number to be left untouched. Young trees of some pine species may develop one or more sets of actively growing buds the same season, but, in any case, the next year several buds normally start from the point where the candles were pruned. Further control is exercised by removing

The record of 38 years. A pine in the Coe collection of bonsai at the Brooklyn Botanic Garden.   COURTESY OF THE BROOKLYN BOTANIC GARDEN

Figure 136. 1925

Figure 137. 1950

Figure 138. 1960

Figure 139. 1963

some or all of these extra buds, and later by shortening the selected candles, in the same way it was done previously.

This method of pruning, by literally nipping new growth in the bud, is applied to most kinds of plants grown as bonsai. In the case of pines, the pruning usually is once a year. In other conifers, such as junipers and cryptomeria, which grow almost continuously, the pruning is repeated continuously. Also, for many deciduous and broadleaf evergreens, grown primarily for their foliage and form, frequent pruning during the growing season is the rule. Examples of the many ways of pruning have been described in Chapter 15, with note of some plant varieties which must be permitted unlimited growth, at certain seasons, in order for them to bear flowers or fruit.

The other method, of renewal pruning to restrain bonsai to fixed or almost stationary limits, is a pruning technique that may be applied both in the dormant and in the active growing seasons, varying according to the growth habits of the plant, and sometimes merely to the convenience of the grower. In its drastic form, renewal pruning removes all of the new growth each year, or even twice in a season, as suggested for willows, lantanas, and others. It is applied to many plants in a slower, more deliberate way, by encouraging new branches from the trunk, or new twigs from the branches, to take the place of branches that are creating too large a periphery for the plant. In this way it is used, also, to replace old wood no longer capable of producing flowers and fruits after one, two or three years, according to species. It is a technique that can be applied even to pines, to some degree, by training active twigs on the side of branches to become the new terminal growth of the branch.

LEAF PRUNING—REDUCING LEAF SIZE

Pruning to control the size of the plant also influences the size of the leaves. Though the most important time in bonsai is when a plant with naturally small leaves was selected in the first place, there often also is an impressive degree of healthy leaf-size reduction that comes as a plant is trained to a ramifying branch structure with many twigs, the result of selective nipping of new growth. Just as a mature tree with many branches and twigs divides its energy into many smaller leaves, instead of the few large ones that are characteristic of the vigorous seedling, so the bonsai trained to the same mature pattern produces smaller leaves.

Leaf size, however, also is directly proportional to the amount of nutrients and water supplied at the moment by the roots or stored within the plant. The first leaves of spring, produced by the food stored late the previous season, for instance, often are considerably larger than those that follow. Occasionally, the reverse is true; if growth the previous year resulted in less food storage, or if pruning depleted it, the first leaves may be smaller than those that grow later, when the roots benefit from the greater supply of food made available as the soil warms and bacterial action releases more nutrients. These larger leaves that occur on some plants, early or late in the season, obviously are ones to be removed.

Thinning the foliage is important as grooming for many bonsai, to maintain a neat appearance and balanced proportions. Often thinning is used to create a more delicate, airy quality, or to reveal the lines of trunks and branches, or to maintain the planes of foliage that show, or suggest, the branch structure. The most extreme degree of leaf pruning is the Japanese practice of removing all or most of the leaves of such plants as maples, crab apples, and zelkova, already described in the last chapter. Notable is that all of these pruning practices involving reduction in the number of leaves on a plant also restrain its capacity to manufacture food, and thus, to grow larger.

OTHER FACTORS INFLUENCING GROWTH AND HEALTH

In addition to pruning, there are other techniques and environmental factors of importance, some of them usefully employed to maintain healthy bonsai, others involving risk unless skillfully controlled.

WATER – Limiting the amount of water to a plant will certainly check growth, and if carried a little further will create an unhealthy weakening of the plant, even though the result is not immediately fatal. However, there are cases where experts use this means to control such flowering trees as apples, apricots, pears, and peaches, which are prone to very strong growth in spring. If pruning alone were relied upon to limit these rapidly lengthening branches, flower buds would be sacrificed. By keeping the plants somewhat dry during this period of the year it is possible to hold branch development to more easily managed lengths. This is a method that should be used with caution.

A special technique in watering—spraying or syringing—by wetting the stems, leaves and trunks repeatedly, more frequently in fact than the soil in the pot is watered, is very helpful in stimulating bud and stem growth, especially of newly transplanted bonsai. It also helps keep plants healthy in hot, dry weather by refreshing the foliage and cleansing it of dust or city grime and, in some instances, of insects. On the other hand, plants that are apt to grow too exuberantly should not be syringed, especially in spring.

FOOD – All plants require a number of mineral elements to maintain health, although the amounts seem infinitesimal. Starving bonsai is an unsafe and unsatisfactory way of controlling growth. An attempt is made in the next chapter to indicate the line between a healthy diet and overindulgence.

LIGHT – Both the kind of growth and its direction are strongly influenced by sunlight, the source of energy for all green plants. When light is weak, plant cells in the stems elongate, leaves are widely spaced; in extreme cases of shade, the stems become so weak and

Figure 140. Watering bonsai is important, not alone to supply this vital element, but also as an aid in controlling insects and disease when the water is applied in a forceful spray.

thin that they cannot support themselves. This lengthening of the individual cells also causes the shady side of the stem to become longer, thus turning the point of growth in the direction of the major source of light. The tamarisk shown in Figures 86–89 is an example of the direction of the light being combined with wiring, to create a wind-blown effect. For a brief period in spring, this plant was located so that it faced sunlight and a bright area of sky, but on the other side was backed by a dark, shady place. There is danger in this kind of treatment, if prolonged, as it can lead to the weakening or death of parts of a plant.

For health, bonsai should be placed where there is reasonably good light on all sides, or in lieu of such a location, plants should be turned from time to time, to maintain a balance.

With good light, plant cells are blocky instead of lanky and lean, stems are thick and strong, leaves closely spaced. The amount of light required by a plant varies with the species. Pines, pomegranates, and most flowering and fruiting kinds thrive on a maximum amount of sunlight, while others, like azaleas, need much less. For sturdy, naturally compact plants, however, it is obvious that the optimum is desirable. The problem this poses for the bonsai grower is that maximum light is best, but also demands more frequent attention to watering. In practice, bonsai usually are given some shade, particularly in the summer, to minimize the danger of drying. But it should be remembered that there is no substitute for adequate light; if time permits more frequent watering, more light should be given.

Natural light is vital to plants, but the unnaturally portable nature of bonsai should not be allowed to be their undoing: Plants should not be moved suddenly from shade to sun. Fatal wilting or foliage burn can be the result. Plants need to be accustomed gradually to strong light. The other move, from sun to shade, does not involve the same hazard. Sudden changes of location, however, in some cases, may result in a plant dropping its flower buds or fruit.

AIR – Fresh-air circulation is essential to healthy growth—even a certain amount of wind is good—for hardy plants of the kinds most commonly grown as bonsai. If plants are to benefit from this air movement, as well as to get balanced light, they should not be crowded into corners, placed too close to walls, or covered by low overhanging foliage. Absence of this free circulation of air becomes a negative factor that results in such liabilities as disease, insects, and poor growth.

EMERGENCY TREATMENT

When, from neglect or less obvious causes, a plant droops or loses good foliage color there can be need for emergency treatment. For plants, unfortunately, there is no shot of adrenalin, no oxygen tent to be called into use. Nor is the usual application of fertilizer of help for a plant that is languid. The practical remedy is to give such a plant good nursing care, under the best of growing conditions. The usual treatment employed by bonsai growers is to remove the plant carefully from its pot, with a minimum of disturbance to the roots, and to put it, preferably, in a ground bed, or if that is not possible, in a larger shallow box of soil. When moved to the ground bed, shade should be provided to give the plant about the same amount of light it had previously. Later, more or less light can be allowed, according to need. Spraying the foliage and branches, from time to time, often helps at first, but care should be employed not to overwater the soil. Nor should the ground bed be allowed to become too dry.

Resort to a ground bed for reviving plants need not be considered a confession of failure. Experts often resort to this kind of rest-cure treatment, especially for delicate plants, or those that are pushing the limits of their normal life span. It is not unheard of for a Japanese bonsaiman to give an old plant a sabbatical year in the ground.

Chapter 17

Watering, Feeding, Root Pruning, Avoiding Pests

The routine care of bonsai involves a daily check most of the year for moisture needs, an occasional feeding, repotting once in a one-to-five-year span, a few simple precautions to keep plants healthy, and attention to a pruning schedule. The total expenditure of time and effort is somewhat less than for a pet, more than for a philodendron.

Neglect pruning for months, or fall behind in the repotting schedule for a year or so and the damage can be repaired. But fail to water a plant in a small pot exposed to hot, dry weather for one full day and the result can be fatal. Watering may be a leisurely and pleasant ritual, or a fleeting chore; it need not be a lengthy operation. I timed myself in the watering of 306 plants (not all bonsai) within reach of a fifty-foot length of hose, and found the daily required time—nine minutes.

It is customarily said that it takes years to master the art of watering plants, and for some of the niceties, this is doubtless true. Most of the variations in the needs of different plants at different times, however, are not difficult to understand through the application of common sense. In the life process of plants, roots take up water from the soil, transmit it to the leaves, which manufacture food and return part of the moisture to the roots, but at the same time, transpire much of the water into the atmosphere, especially in sunny weather. From this we may deduce—and will soon observe—that:

Soil with many roots in it, such as pot-bound plants, dry out quickly; soil with few roots in it, as in recently repotted plants, stay moist longer.

Plants require more water on bright days than on dull days, even in winter.

Plants need more moisture during rapid growth, less when foliage is mature, and least during dormancy.

Plants with large leaves, as a rule, need more water than those with small, or needled, foliage.

In practice even this understanding need not be applied analytically to each plant each day. If the potting soil has a structure that assures good drainage, it is almost impossible to overwater. The rule, then, is water thoroughly every day during the growing season. Check even after a summer rain, because it may be found that not enough fell on the small exposed soil surface in the pot to moisten it throughout. If in doubt, give more water. Plants may require more than once-a-day watering. In the beginning it is prudent to check their condition several times a day, if possible, to see how quickly they become dry. And then spot-check, in different seasons, to see how the pattern of variations develops under these differing conditions.

Plants that the next day seem wilted or too dry will need more water or more frequent watering. Sometimes alterations of the environment can bring their requirements back to once-a-day schedule, and some possibilities in this line are touched on in the next chapter.

Beware the advice often given to houseplant growers "Don't water again until the soil becomes dry" unless you recognize that "dry" does not mean totally dry. If the soil in a pot is allowed to become really dry, only plants with special adaption to desert conditions will survive in it. For health of soil and plants there needs to be an interchange of water and air in the soil structure, from the saturated period when thoroughly watered, to the state where air has re-entered the pore space of the soil, even though it still contains some moisture. In cool, damp climates care should be taken not to overwater, by allowing the soil to achieve this "somewhat dry" condition periodically. For hot weather anywhere, and especially in areas where the humidity may drop very low, the policy should be to take extreme precaution to see that bonsai, in small pots, are adequately watered. Failure to water sufficiently during dry weather kills more bonsai than any other cause.

Water when bonsai needs it, no matter what time that may be. I emphasize this in particular, because of the widespread advice not to water plants in sunshine. If the plant shows distress, or the soil feels very dry, don't wait until sundown. Though many practices in the art of plant growing continue to prove practical whether explained scientifically or not, the particular bit of garden folklore, about not watering plants in sunshine, has little evidence to support it.

It is true that wetting the foliage of some plants seems to increase the spread of disease; as examples, blackspot on roses in the East, leaf blights of soft, hairy foliage of some begonias. Watering late in the day so the plant remains wet all night is favorable for disease in certain plants, and promotes damping-off of cuttings and seedlings. Very cold water, I know by experiment, can damage the leaves of African violets, varying according to varieties, while tepid water, under the same circumstances, is not harmful.

The usual explanation of the damage done by wetting leaves in sunlight is that it burns them, and the most ingenious explanation I have read is that the drops of water form little lenses that focus the rays of the sun on the foliage. Whatever the hazard ascribed, the present-day practice of professional growers discounts it. Many millions of plants, of most if not all the varieties generally grown as bonsai, are regularly watered in full sunlight by nurserymen. In some of the hottest parts of this country, there are to my knowledge nurserymen who follow the practice of watering daily by overhead irrigation, applying water, as a rule, for one hour to plants in gallon containers; for two hours to those in larger containers. The timing is based on the availability of labor and water pressure in the various parts of the nursery, not on the sunlight. Countless cuttings are rooted by professionals under intermittent mist, which keeps the foliage almost constantly wet, in full or almost full sunlight. I have asked directors of botanic gardens, horticultural supervisors of public parks, and many nurserymen about watering plants in sunlight; all of them that I have talked to have told me they have heard of the advice but none of them pay any attention to it. I have no evidence so far that watering burns foliage any more than it burns the skin of my grandchildren when they play under the sprinkler on the lawn. Water cools foliage, rather than the reverse. I know bonsai growers who spray their plants deliberately to refresh them during very hot weather.

FEEDING

Perhaps basic advice to those American gardeners who are conditioned to a land of overabundance is: use restraint in feeding bonsai. Fertilizer for plants, often called "plant food," is not a counterpart to the food we ingest. Plants manufacture their own food largely from the elements in water, air, and sunlight; the nutrients absorbed through their roots amount to little more than what to us would be considered a vitamin and mineral supplement. These are vital, but needed in minute amounts only. Ordinarily, potting soil will provide all that is required for a considerable period of time, sometimes from one repotting to the next. One Japanese friend of mine, a professional plant grower for more than half a century, expressed his experience this way: "I have seen plants watered to death, dried to death, and fed to death, but never one starved to death." Of course, it is possible for a plant to starve, but the case is indeed a rarity and other factors usually are involved. Care and environmental conditions should be checked first if a plant seems unhealthy, because feeding seldom is of benefit to a plant that languishes.

The elements ordinarily absorbed by plants through their roots—mainly nitrogen, phosphorus, and potash—are available in this country in several forms convenient for feeding bonsai. These include the relatively odorless and completely soluble fertilizers that are applied to the soil in dilute solutions. In some cases this is sold as a concentrate solution, such as the fish emulsions especially popular on the West Coast. Others are dry chemical formulations to be mixed with water, and several have been on the market for many years, for use on houseplants in particular. Of recent times they have been suggested for foliar application; i.e., feeding plants through their leaves and stems by applying a solution to these upper parts. These and dry organic fertilizers were discussed in some detail in Chapter 11.

A simplified feeding program, based on soluble fertilizers mixed at one half to one fourth the usual recommended strength and applied as a thorough watering of the soil, might be the following:

In early spring, one application to all plants that have not been repotted, especially to those that are approaching a root-bound condition or are suspected of needing repotting.

After the start of healthy new spring growth, one or more feedings to plants in which growth is to be encouraged; in particular, plants in training.

In summer, after spring growth has matured, one or more feedings.

In autumn, just before and as leaves start to fall from deciduous trees, one or more feedings, perhaps of a slightly stronger solution.

Such a program perhaps would be suitable where the basic soil is poor, and, even then—it should be noted—very dilute solutions are indicated. There is much greater danger in overfeeding than in underfeeding. This is the experience of many of the better growers in this country who follow a policy of not feeding at all until plants have become well established after repotting, and then using only slow-acting organic fertilizers.

Within a collection, plants should be treated according to their needs, deviating to whatever degree thought wise from the standard program. In general, needled trees need much less feeding than other plants. Flowering and fruiting bonsai require the most feeding, and are usually greatly helped by the frequent application of very dilute fertilizer during the periods that the buds and fruit form. Some growers do this on a once-a-week basis. *Mame* bonsai and any plant in a minimum of soil, or pot bound, needs more frequent and careful feeding to maintain healthy vigor.

It is practical, also, to use dry organic fertilizers, such as cottonseed meal or dehydrated manures, applied as top dressings to the soil, and then watered in thoroughly. Manures and sometimes unleached wood ashes are mixed in water, and then used in a weak solution, as another method of application. It is common practice to allow the manure to stand in a container of water for several days, with occasional stirrings, before use; then, a portion is further diluted in the watering can. A few growers I know, recognizing the gray zone of inexact knowledge of feeding requirements, follow a policy of alternating the use of different kinds of fertilizer.

In general, it may be said that the soluble chemical fertilizers give quick stimulation, even in cold soil of early spring, but produce a short-term effect. Dry organic plant foods, mixed with the potting soil or applied as a top dressing, release their nutrients slowly over a long period.

Feeding practices vary tremendously among growers in this country, and such differences can be understandably successful in view of the wide variations in basic soil and the needs of plants. Some hobbyists feed with a very dilute solution almost every week during the growing seasons. Others only once or twice, in summer and fall. I have noted cases where azaleas, camellias, and pines have done very well without feeding at all from one repotting to the next.

REPOTTING AND ROOT PRUNING

Repotting bonsai is such a seeming negation of the common American practice of repotting plants into larger and larger containers that it deserves special note. Fortunately, there is nothing particularly difficult about it, except perhaps to bring ourselves to believe that it is entirely practical to maintain a plant in good health in the same size container almost indefinitely.

The frequency of repotting is adjusted to a schedule that meets the

Root pruning makes room for new soil and healthy root growth. Step by step:

Figure 141. Save moss if present.

Figure 142. Roots of a pot-bound plant hold the soil in a solid mass.

Figure 143. Loosen soil and roots around edges with a pointed stick or pencil.

Figure 144. Prune roots about one third around the sides.

Figure 145. Trim roots close to soil underneath.

needs of a particular plant, to provide an opportunity to replace old soil that has become worn out through continued use, and to maintain a healthy balance of root structure to the top branching of the plant. Most species are more favorably repotted near the end of the dormant period in mild climates; elsewhere toward the end of winter, just as growth starts. For varieties considered sensitive to the cold of a particular climate, and for the true subtropicals, repotting should be delayed a little until growth begins to show, as a general rule. A few species that bloom in winter or very early spring may be repotted to advantage either in early autumn or immediately after the flowers begin to wither.

The frequency of repotting depends on the needs of the plant—any kind requires it as the plant becomes thoroughly pot bound, which may be noted by a thick matting of fine roots around the outer edge of the root ball when the plant is turned out of the container. Pines and most needled evergreens make more compact growth when repotted infrequently, perhaps once in three to five years, or even less often. Fruiting and flowering trees and *mame* bonsai are usually repotted each year. And in the case of the exceptions noted previously, a few kinds may be repotted more than once in a year.

Repotting, step by step:

Figure 146. Screen wire and fine gravel to assure drainage.

Figure 147. Potting stick firms granular soil around roots.

Figure 148. Rubber-covered wire loop to pin down a wayward root.

Figure 149. Fine topsoil smoothed with a brush.

Figure 150. Repotting complete, plant is watered, then pruned.

Repotting follows closely the method for the first potting, described in Chapter 12. Pick a shady, sheltered place for the work, and have all materials and tools needed immediately at hand, so the roots need not be exposed any longer than necessary.

If the fingers of one hand are placed over the surface of the soil, with the trunk emerging between them, and the pot turned upside down and tapped lightly on a hard surface, the complete root ball usually will slip easily from the pot. If not, it may be necessary to loosen the roots and soil around the edges of the container with a metal hook or old screwdriver, and then proceed in the same manner. A pot-bound plant will hold the soil in one solid mass with its matted roots. The first step in replacing part of this soil and pruning the roots is to loosen the roots and soil on the outer edges and below, with hook or potting stick, allowing the soil to fall away. The amount of soil replacement advisable varies with the plant and purpose, but in general about one third is enough, although in some cases as much as two thirds might be removed.

Roots are trimmed with sharp pruners around the periphery of the mass and across the bottom. Some growers consider it good practice to allow the roots to hang downward, and then trim them with a cut parallel to the bottom of the pot, thus encouraging a spreading, shallow pattern of new root formation. Roots growing outward from the trunk may be permitted to extend somewhat beyond the zone of old soil. Roots growing downward normally are trimmed short. The purpose of pruning, of course, is to allow space for new soil and new root growth, but the larger roots that are so plainly visible, and that are pruned at repotting, are mainly used by the plant for anchorage and for food storage, rather than for directly absorbing moisture and nutrients. This function is carried out by tiny root hairs that, in most species, are almost invisible. As new roots grow, these fine root hairs extend outward between the soil particles. During favorable conditions, they are in rapid, active growth. When the soil is too cold, too hot, too dry, or too wet, these root hairs die, and then are replaced at the next time of growth.

How much should roots be pruned? As a general rule, the pruning should be to the extent that a space is allowed for new soil about one fourth to one third the distance from the edge of the pot toward the trunk. Unless carried too far, the greater the pruning, the more new growth response will result, especially from vigorous kinds of plants. Sturdy, rapid growers, like willow and lantana, can be as roughly handled as to use a hatchet to chop off the outer root mass by a third or more. Loosening the soil and trimming more conservatively is the better method, however. Old plants, those that are slow growing by nature, and those in a weakened condition, should be pruned less drastically.

Is the old soil at the base of the trunk never replaced? It is not necessary for a long time, and it is attended with some hazard if attempted on old plants and those that resent transplanting. One way to undertake it with safety is to remove a pie-shaped section of old soil, loosening it carefully with a slender potting stick, and then carefully repacking new soil around the roots. In this manner, by choosing different quadrants in succession, a change may be carried out over a period of years.

As at the time of the first potting, previously described, the plant should be thoroughly watered and then put in a sheltered place for a few days. Until growth starts, overwatering should be avoided. It is well to direct the water to the base of the trunk, in order to keep the old soil containing the roots properly moist, but avoid saturating the new soil with too great frequency.

AVOIDING PESTS

Although plants, as bonsai, are susceptible to all the pests and diseases peculiar to their species when grown in large size, I have found these small plants relatively trouble-free. In part, this is because ordinary care balks some pests; for instance, forceful spraying of foliage with the hose while watering is often all the control necessary for certain spider mites and aphids, and some forms of mildew disease. The placement of these portable plants in raised positions helps to forestall some hazards, and makes it easy for almost-daily close inspection to reveal a pest before it can do widespread damage; countermeasures are easy and effective at this stage.

Avoiding plant troubles is easier than curing them. Prevention is almost the only means to control plant disease, and this often requires no more than that a healthy environment be maintained, with special attention to adequate light and good air circulation. Insect pests usually can be quickly halted when first seen, though the better way here, too, is in prevention. Plants on raised benches are removed from many of the crawling pests, and infrequent use of an insecticidal spray handles the most dangerous ones that might reach them. Once a year or so, I spray the ground areas where plants are kept, as well as the soil beneath plant benches, with a solution of chlordane, and in this way eliminate the problem of crawling pests, including ants that bring aphids and sometimes diseases to plants.

I have found little need for poisonous sprays, but for the rare occasions there are particularly effective ones available. These include the prepared mixtures usually called "floral sprays," compounded to protect shrubs and flowering plants, rather than vegetables. Some effective ones contain combinations of malathion, lindane and DDT or DDD or methoxychlor. Once a year I spray the entire bonsai area at our home with such a spray, using a hose-end attachment. For individual plants or small collections, a simple flit gun will serve. Even the inexpensive plunger-type plastic spray, operated with one finger —sold for spraying window cleaner—is useful.

In some areas of the country regular spraying or dusting is required, to control pests or disease of certain species. Information on this should be sought from experienced growers or nurserymen. A note of warning might be sounded for the beginner about a few pests that may not be noticed until damage is extensive, or with which the symptoms are easily misread. Among these are the spider mites that are so small they are difficult to see. The standard test is to place a piece of white paper beneath a branch, tap the leaves, and then examine the specks that are shown on the paper. If the specks crawl, or if they smear when rubbed with the finger tip, you may assume you have mites present. These actually are tiny, eight-legged arachnids, kin of spiders, and not insects. The usual visible symptom caused by them is a yellowing, speckling, or declining healthy color of the foliage. When damage has advanced this far it often is slow to be repaired by new growth. It is well to spray species known to be susceptible to mites. I follow this policy of two or three sprays a season, applied thoroughly to the underside of the leaves, in particular, to control the common pests in my area of azaleas, camellias, and citrus varieties. Scale insects are also difficult to control, and special attention should be given them at the first appearance. At one period of the year some species are noticeable when the tiny, white males swarm on the underside of leaves or on stems. Most of the time scale insects appear as brown or black bumps, sometimes shaped like oyster shells that do not move.

A final uninvited guest that may seem mysterious is sooty mold, a kind of fungus growth that forms a blackish covering on the foliage of some plants. This is not harmful in itself, but is disfiguring. It is caused by a mold on the excretions of certain small insects. If the mold forms on lower leaves of your plants, spray your bonsai for insects, not the disease. If the mold forms on the upper parts of your bonsai, spray foliage of trees growing overhead, or move your plants. The mold can be washed off with soap and water.

The most serious pests that may damage bonsai are not insects and disease, but animals, birds, and people. This may range from the injury inflicted by the beach ball thrown by the neighbor's children, to the unplanned pruning undertaken by rabbits and mice. For human and rabbit pests, the only sure barrier I know about is a fence; in the case of the latter four-footed pests, a tight wire mesh. Birds are an ornament in the garden and a help in the biological control of many insects, but they can be a nuisance to the owner of a bonsai collection, by removing moss from the soil in bonsai pots and by eating berries or, sometimes, even the flowers on specimen plants. Some bird species collect moss for use in their nests, but the most frequent damage I have had is from their lifting pieces of moss in their search for insects.

Sometimes they pick up small plants, as well as moss, and fling them aside in their diligent search for food. A physical barrier of screen or mesh is the only certain control. For plants with particularly handsome moss, sometimes I have provided protection with a small individual wire cage, made of one-inch poultry netting.

Mice are most likely to be a problem during the winter months when plants are kept in a shed or a deep cold frame. Ordinary wire will keep rabbits out of such places, but mice are difficult to exclude. My practice has been to put out special baits for mice, in containers that will keep them out of the reach of birds, in storage areas a week or two before putting plants in those places. Rabbits may also prove damaging in the winter season for plants in ground beds, and they are difficult to stop with anything short of a wire fence with the bottom sunk into the soil. Although their tastes are unpredictable, they have proved particularly attracted, in my area, to certain hollies, barberries, maples, and flowering apricots.

Chapter 18

Adapting Bonsai to Your Home,
Your Climate

Healthy bonsai that require a minimum of special attention are the
result of action by their owners—in one of two ways or their combination. They are: (1) selecting plants adapted to the particular climate,
to one's particular home; or, (2) modifying the immediate environment and the effects of climate to meet the requirements of the
plants. There are practical limits in modifying to suit the plants, but
these changes are much more easily made for portable specimens in
containers than they are for plants in the garden. When the needs
of the plants are considered, if thought is given at the same time to
the convenience and pleasure of the gardener, then the necessary attention more certainly will be accorded them.

Simply stated, most bonsai are outdoor potted plants that usually
require some protection from the extremes of weather, summer, or
winter. In cold climates the winter protection of a deep cold frame
or a cool greenhouse is ideal for the hardy species; the tropical and
subtropical varieties become houseplants, requiring reasonable attention to their needs for light and humidity. In hot climates the
emphasis is on summer protection, perhaps by use of a lath house to
moderate intense sunshine, and screens to deflect dry winds. The effective care of bonsai in this country usually has proved neither
seriously complicated nor overly simple. Some hobbyists, for instance,
have no winter problem at all, while others in cold climates have
solved it easily by burying the pots in the soil of their gardens. In
summer a congenial place for plants may be on a garden wall in the
partial shade of tall trees, or on a terrace on the lee side of the house.
Difficult problems of climate, perhaps more extreme than bonsaimen
in Japan encounter, have been solved with ingenuity by growers in the
various parts of this country.

The Japanese way of caring for bonsai most frequently described is
to keep the plants on benches or tables outdoors in summer and, for

Selecting plants suitable to the climate makes the care of bonsai a simpler matter. Native junipers and pines are good choices for the hot dry areas.

Figure 151a. Juniper, 16 inches.

the hardy species, in an open shed in winter. Although the climate of the islands that make up Japan ranges from subarctic tundras in the north to areas where oranges grow in the south, the zone that produces these recommendations is the vicinity of Tokyo, about midway between the extremes. The weather there, in general, is profoundly influenced by two factors: (1) Japan has a marine climate, moderated by large bodies of water. (2) It is in a part of the world where monsoons create a definite rain pattern. At the start of summer in Tokyo, when heat and drought come to many parts of the United States, the summer monsoon brings a period of heavy rainfall, a time of dampness and muddiness that has given rise to the use of raised steppingstones and moss in the characteristic Japanese garden. In winter another monsoon, laden with less moisture, brings snows and cold from the icy land mass of Siberia. Japan has its violent extremes, of typhoon and tidal wave, but little of drought, drying winds, and the extremes of heat and cold that characterize much of the North American continent, especially in the great area between the Rockies and the Appalachians, where torrid heat from the south and frigid air from the north move unimpeded. The humidity of the Japanese marine climate also moderates temperatures, in contrast to the wide variation within a single day in areas of our Southwest, where clear,

Figure 151b. Pinion pine, 38 inches. DON JIM, HOLLYWOOD

dry air permits full absorption of heat from the sun in the day, and as readily permits the dissipation of this stored heat by radiation at night. The only rough counterpart of a "Japanese climate" in this country is restricted to coastal areas of the Northwest and on the eastern seaboard.

FOR THOSE WITHOUT WINTERS, WITHOUT GARDENS

Special restrictions apply to bonsai growers in this country who live in apartments without access to outdoor garden space, and to hobbyists in climatic zones without a definite winter season. Species of plants that require a cold dormant period are not adapted to Hawaii and Florida, and may be of limited use in southern California and the Rio Grande Valley in Texas. The restriction is not much of a handicap, as indicated through the wide variety of plants successfully grown by skilled bonsaimen in Hawaii and the warmer parts of California. While a few popular species are eliminated, these are more than made up for by the addition of many less common ornamental plants. The problems in these areas of pleasant, mild climate are more apt to be related to matters of soil and localized pests. A grower in

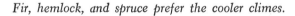

Fir, hemlock, and spruce prefer the cooler climes.

Figure 152. Hemlock, 7 inches.

Hawaii mentions heavy soil that needs lightening for good drainage. In Florida the soil may prove almost pure sand. In both cases, adjusting the soil for potted plants need not be a major problem. In all these warmer zones, however, shading plants from intense sunshine is important.

The city dweller must meet handicaps with considerable determination if he is to grow traditional bonsai in an apartment. Even common houseplants find it difficult enough to tolerate continuous life in the peculiar indoor climate of the average American home, where there is the combination of perpetual spring temperatures, gloom of winter, and the dry air of the desert. A few tropicals, chosen from

A bonsai-style of potting often makes small houseplants more decorative. Like many other tender species grown as houseplants, these thrive in a sheltered place outdoors in summer, then come indoors for the cold months.

Figure 153. Mistletoe fig (*Ficus diversifolia*), 5 inches.

Figure 154. Three-year-old seedling Norfolk Island pine (*Araucaria excelsa*), 7 inches.

those that survive on dark forest floors and must endure periodic droughts, can take this paradoxical combination, but these, in most instances, are foliage plants that lack the sturdy stature of bonsai. The limitation mainly for the indoor gardener, then, is in finding plants that will grow under such conditions. A few houseplants have treelike qualities; one is jade plant (*Crassula* varieties) that develops a massive trunk in old age; another is Norfolk Island pine (*Araucaria excelsa*), that assumes a graceful tree-form as a small plant, but is much too symmetrical and lacking in "grandeur" to fill the role of true bonsai. However, many hobbyists, I find, have created adapted bonsai of houseplant varieties, improving the ornamental character of their plants by using a bonsai style of potting and, in some cases, pruning and wiring.

Able and determined bonsai fanciers do find ways to overcome problems: One, a nurseryman who lives in a three-room apartment in the city, indulges his interest in unusual hardy plants with a fairly large collection, the individual specimens rotated to a place indoors for periods of two to five days. The rest of the time they are kept outdoors. An adjacent courtyard serves this purpose in summer, or for another city dweller, it might be a fire escape or a roof garden. In winter, he tells me that he "boards out" his hardy plants, sinking the pots in the soil in a place where they are protected from the extremes of weather. He lists plants better adapted for longer indoor use as pomegranate, dwarf Japanese holly, and some varieties of citrus.

There are growers who take advantage of the more favorable locations indoors, where light is good and temperatures not too high. Some improve the immediate environment by keeping miniature bonsai collections in small "indoor greenhouses," a kind of modern Wardian case, where humidity can be kept at a high level within the glass enclosure. Prolonged periods in such devices are not necessarily favorable for hardy species, however.

An amateur grower, who likes to display at his office the plants he has grown and trained at his suburban home, has found means to overcome the particularly unfavorable condition in an office building that is closed for the weekend. As a base for plants indoors, he uses large, shallow trays filled with gravel. This is not the traditional Japanese way of showing plants, but the black trays with clean gravel form an attractive background and, at the same time, serve to simplify the watering process, catching any drips that might otherwise damage furniture or the floor. In fact, some water in the gravel is advisable, to add to the humidity in the immediate area. In addition, to meet the problem of dry air, this bonsai-hobbyist business executive also has installed a small humidifying device in this office. Before leaving for home Friday he fills up the humidifier, waters the plants thoroughly, and goes home confident he will find them in good condition Monday morning.

Bonsai provides a way to bring the bright hues of autumn indoors for a brief display.

Figure 155. Maple grove, 25 inches.

MICROCLIMATES

After the selection of the plant, the next step is to find or create in the home or garden a microclimate favorable to its healthy growth. Or sometimes the unalterable limits of the microclimate should be ascertained first, then the plant selected. In any case, "microclimate," so important to the plant, is merely a modern term for what able gardeners have known for a long time—that local conditions of shade, topography, and exposure to wind—the sum of these factors—can spell success or failure in one location against another that may not be far away. Gardeners in England long ago learned that on a warm south wall they could ripen fruits of species which would fail utterly if grown in the open. The climate varies from one side of a house to another.

The microclimate for a plant is important in winter, as well as in summer, when it is dormant, as well as when it is growing. The cases cited below may be considered examples of favorable microclimates for the plants involved.

Winter cold in the North, and in the mountains, is a weather factor of prime importance, because the hardiness of a plant is a relative matter. Move any hardy species to the north far enough, or to an elevation high enough, and it becomes "tender." Plants in containers, if the roots are permitted to freeze at the same low temperatures as the tops, are more sensitive to cold than well-established plants of the same species growing in the ground. Thus, a parasol tree (*Firmiana simplex*) might be rated tender in New York under any circumstance, hardy growing in the ground in Tennessee, but tender to winter cold several hundred miles south in Georgia, if grown in a container fully exposed to the weather.

The most protection against cold, of course, must be provided in areas of severe winters. One expert in a part of New York State, where temperatures regularly drop to twenty degrees below zero, uses a sun-pit to winter all his bonsai. A sun-pit, such as his, is a deeper and larger variation of the usual cold frame. The temperature is kept at mild levels by the heat of the earth, conserved by insulated covering at night, or during cold spells, augmented by sunshine on clear days. Ordinarily, this type of shelter is made large enough to allow the gardener to enter via steps, so plants can be handled more easily. In this particular case, all deciduous bonsai are stored under shelves, stacked close together, partially on top of each other to save space. The evergreen ones are set on the shelves where they get light on sunny days when the screens are off the pit. Usually, there is no freezing within the pit. Although after a long period of zero weather it may get down to freezing along the edges, the soil in the pots is never frozen solid. Plants are watered occasionally as they become dry.

In spring, when the plants are first brought out, there always is a watching period, for they are usually farther advanced in growth than the regular vegetation outdoors, and if a hard freeze is expected, these potted plants are returned to cover overnight.

Plants in this particular case are all hardy species, including some exotics, such as Japanese maples and zelkovas, but most of them natives, such as pitch pine; hemlock; balsam fir; red, white, and black spruce; juniper; hornbeams; and American larch.

One of the most notable collections of old bonsai has been kept at the Arnold Arboretum near Boston, where winter temperatures normally go to five or ten degrees below zero, occasionally as low as a minus-thirty degrees. The plants, imported by the then ambassador to Japan, Larz Anderson, in 1912, before the plant quarantine was enacted, include such hardy varieties as Hinoki cypress, Japanese maples, flowering cherries, five-needle pine, and larch. For many years the Larz Anderson collection spent the winter in a pit house seven feet deep. Recently a building has been constructed for winter storage where temperatures can be controlled by heat and, if need be, by refrigeration. The bonsai share space there with other plants, some of which are given special protection to prevent their premature growth in early spring, a condition that often results in damage or loss. The temperature does not go much below thirty degrees in winter. In summer the bonsai are placed on display in a lath house.

A very extensive collection of bonsai, of many species and kinds, hardy and tender ones, is maintained at the Brooklyn Botanic Garden in New York. Some of the specimens were acquired as donations as early as 1925, many others are more recent acquisitions. As they are a special feature of this arboretum, different plants are moved into position for display periodically. In summer several favorable locations are used to maintain plants in healthy condition. Some bonsai are kept on tables; others in ground beds, in full sun; many others are partially shaded in lath houses. A few are kept in lightly shaded and well-ventilated greenhouses.

In winter, protection is according to need. Most hardy species are kept in deep cold frames, sunk below frost line in the soil. Eight inches of gravel in the bottom provides good drainage. Walls of the pits are insulated. Overhead sash is made of plastic fastened to both sides of wooden frames, thus providing an air space for insulation against cold. As with any garden frame containing plants, these are carefully watched to see that they do not overheat in bright weather, and are watered as the plants require it.

Tropical plants are kept in a cool greenhouse, which also houses many of the hardy species as well, in particular the very small bonsai, or types with roots exposed over rocks. Both of these kinds are more quickly damaged by neglect or unfavorable weather.

If care is taken to provide adequate ventilation and prevent overheating, the cool greenhouse is about the ideal for all hardy species, because while these plants need a cold period for normal dormancy, very few, if any, require actual freezing. A range of forty to fifty degrees, for two months or so, is usually adequate. Such a cool greenhouse also is a good place for citrus varieties, for camellias that bloom in winter, and for azaleas that will bloom in late winter or early spring. Some hobbyists I know enjoy these attractive plants in a cool greenhouse that also protects their bonsai.

Elaborate and expensive equipment is not necessary, however. One hobbyist, in an area where winter temperatures often go to ten below zero, has a simple method of year-around protection. In summer he keeps his plants on a steplike arrangement of shelves in the open garden, partially shaded by tall trees. In former years he removed all hardy plants from their pots in autumn, "planted" them in the garden, then protected them further with a mulch of oak leaves and pine needles. Of recent years he has simply placed his hardy plants under the stairstep table, mulched them heavily with leaves, and then covered the whole contrivance with burlap. This is an area of fairly heavy snows, so it is not necessary to check on the moisture needs of his plants very often.

This grower keeps his tender, tropical varieties in an attic room that is insulated but not heated. Light is admitted to the room by a window, near which he keeps a large table equipped with a metal tray. Plants stand in gravel in this tray, where they may be conveniently watered.

Another bonsai fancier in a cold area uses a lean-to shelter, built against the house, protected by double plastic panels fitted in place in winter. A small heater keeps plants from hard frost. Deciduous varieties that require very little light are stored under the shelves. Evergreens are placed on the upper levels. Tropical varieties are kept in the house, located near windows, or a cooler enclosed porch, where light conditions are to their liking. A small humidifier is used to make indoor conditions even more congenial for the plants.

Within the limited space of our own small garden, in a zone where zero is experienced infrequently, I use five areas of differing microclimates for potted plants in winter. A few of the hardiest bonsai (some pines, for instance) are left in exposed positions on shelves or tables. Most of the hardy species are moved to a position on ground beds, usually immediately below the tabletops, which are dismantled in winter. The ground slants slightly, to assure drainage, and is covered with gravel, on which the pots rest. A low wall of loose brick, front and back, controls wind to some extent in this sheltered area. In a few cases, plants are removed from their pots and set in an earth bed, then lightly mulched with pine needles. Another place for outdoor storage is a cold frame built of concrete blocks, two feet deep, with a thick layer of crushed rock in the bottom for drainage. The frame faces south, and the north side of it is banked with earth. Some smaller plants are kept here, and a few in more valuable pots. Usually the only shelter given them is a lath screen, used mainly to shade the plants against overheating during sunny periods in winter.

All tropical and some hardy ones are kept in a cool lean-to greenhouse, with the thermostat set for heat to come on when the temperature drops to thirty-five. By opening overhead vents on warm days, we try to keep the temperature down to fifty throughout the winter. Electronic controls, to operate these vents automatically, would be a convenience. In addition, a few plants are kept in our house on the floor near a glass wall in the living room that faces east.

FOR SUMMER PLEASURE

As we move in this country from north to south, from east to west, the time of special problems in many places is summer, and in some areas where winter is the difficult season, cold may not be the only factor. Winter is long and relatively cold in Denver, for instance, but protecting hardy plants by burying them partially in the ground may not be the only protection; the bonsai grower there may need to check for moisture needs in winter with greater care than his eastern counterpart. The effect of drying winds in the Mid and Far West is hard for a gardener in the humid East to comprehend without experiencing it. Sunshine that penetrates the clear air in the West with 90 per cent efficiency also is incredibly strong—and potentially damaging—in contrast to sunshine that reaches the earth, in less than half the amount, in the eastern states.

Shade from hot afternoon sun in particular is important, and the controlled shade of a lath house is favored in the West. Equally important, in most places, is some kind of barrier to the prevailing wind, provided by fence, wall, or ornamental screen.

Gardeners in the warm zones have been the pioneers in developing

Figure 156. A lath house proves to be a healthy place for this venerable specimen of trident maple to spend the summer.

outdoor-living space, with their typical garden rooms in Florida, lanais and patios in the Southwest. Thought and artistry have been employed to make these places more comfortable for people, with results that often are also more favorable for plants. Bonsai fanciers on the West Coast, in particular, have shown taste and skill in developing outdoor areas pleasantly habitable for both plants and man. Shade sometimes is provided by conventional wooden lath, spaced equally by its own width, to reduce by half the intensity of the sun, or by special aluminum lath that is angled to give most shade in the hottest period, but less shade early or late. Sometimes ornamental wooden framing is used overhead, or panels fitted with plastic netting. Shelter from wind is afforded by projecting walls, by fences of rustic redwood grape stakes or translucent plastic, or by panels which may be freestanding as background for bonsai.

Low humidity compounds the problem of hot sun and wind, especially in many parts of the Southwest, where there is no rain whatsoever during the summer months. Ingenuity has been used to combat this dry air, often with mechanical watering devices. A few hobbyists have humidifiers similar to those used in orchid greenhouses, but the most common way is to rig up a watering device and have it timed to turn on the water for an occasional cooling bath, with the water sprayed up over the bonsai plants from a misting nozzle. One grower in a California valley where there is no summer rain, has such an arrangement that waters the plants for ten minutes in the early morning, again for five minutes in the late afternoon. He supplements this with hand watering of those individual plants which seem to require it. Another grower has employed the spray nozzles of the kind used in supermarkets to keep vegetables fresh.

Mist sprays, or other methods of watering results in a much cooler, more congenial condition in the immediate area, if the humidity is very low. This result is particularly noticeable when combined with some shade.

It is here, I should point out, that the American growers who I have sensed were most pleased with bonsai are those who have brought the plants into their daily life, in areas of outdoor living, where they may be seen and enjoyed frequently; where the plants are displayed to advantage; and where they may be cared for with a minimum of inconvenience. In a collection, no doubt there will be individual plants worthy of special note at certain seasons. But bonsai are not enjoyed to the fullest if single specimens are trotted out briefly, like a blooded horse, to be admired, and that is all. Even plants in training are enjoyed the more if thought is given to their locations. Enthusiasts seem to share this view, wherever they may live.

Many growers display plants on terraces or patios, or at the entry, where they are seen and enjoyed frequently every day. Perhaps one or two plants are in position for special display on a terrace table, or a shelf on the wall near the door. Other plants are arranged conveniently in a raised position nearby. One amateur grower has all facilities closely grouped around an outdoor living room next to the house. Chairs are arranged for visitors, and a table for refreshments is decorated with one bonsai. Some bonsai plants are on a wall, others— the small ones—in gravel-filled trays on benches. Nearby, a garden house equipped with a skylight provides space for potting and for recuperation of plants for a few days after wiring. In winter it is a shelter for hardy species.

One garden my wife and I visited has a special patio somewhat detached from the house, partially shaded by fine trees, paved with gravel, equipped with lawn furniture for the owner and guests, and tables for the plants. In this case, iron grillwork in several forms has been used as tabletops, raised to suitable height on blocks, and both blocks and ironwork painted black. Near the patio stands a garden house with tools, a potting bench, and bins of prepared soil.

Plant enthusiasts in cold climates devise a place for their favorites

Hobbyists who enjoy bonsai the most are those who create environments that are congenial for both man and bonsai.

Figure 157. The spruce bonsai here (26 inches tall), decorates an outdoor living-room terrace adjacent to a garden house.

Figure 158. One way to protect small bonsai that are hardy is to shift them, as in the case of this small juniper, from their tiny display pots to larger containers of sand and peat moss. The larger pot lessens the hazard of drying. The juniper, then, might be kept in a deep cold frame or a cool greenhouse for the winter.

in winter. One, a combined living and plant room—in a corner, a raised fireplace with built-in, old-fashioned oven; on one side a broad expanse of glass that offers a view of a wintry scene for many months, and protects plants that are green indoors throughout the year.

A grower in the Northeast has solved both summer and winter

Where the climate is not too severe, the hardiest species enjoy the normal out-door conditions of winter.

Figure 159. A pine is whitened by the first snow.

Figure 160. The screen in the background tempers the wind, and the position of the pots on the ground moderates the cold of the Upper South for these hardy varieties. Many species grown as bonsai, however, require more careful protection in winter.

weather extremes by building a masonry planter, similar to the kind commonly used as part of some house fronts, but in this case taller, for the convenience of the gardener. In the top of this planter a sandy mixture serves as base for the bonsai pots. In summer the containers are sunk about one third into the mixture, a position that slows drying in hot weather. In winter the pots of hardy species are buried in the sand, which is brought up around the base of the trunks. A mulch then completes the protection against cold.

A family with a collection of bonsai in the West has built an extension of lath shading out from the living-dining room. Good design creates interesting shadows, and shades the plants as well. Benches bring plants to within arm's reach, for ease in care and for enjoyment. In some cases, special stands have been devised, with simple panels to offer background for display of the plants, and sturdily anchored to defy the wind—and children.

In all areas, prudence suggests that plants be selected that are reasonably well adapted to the climate. In sections where the summers are cool, and air moist, spruces and firs are the reasonable choice, rather than crape myrtle. In southwestern areas, where the sun is intense, air dry, and perhaps the water laden with minerals, the preference—let us say—should be for pines and native junipers, rather than Japanese maples.

It is true that modifying an environment to make it suitable for living plants often creates a living space more agreeable for the grower. But those who consider bonsai merely as living plants do not understand them to the fullest. The same may be said for those who think of them, primarily, as works of art. Bonsai are both. The amount of attention they require for their living dimension is a small price to pay for the reward they confer.

Reference

GLOSSARY

Adapted bonsai – a term applied to container plants which have had their picturesque qualities enhanced by a bonsai style of potting and usually some pruning, but which normally are not given the careful training and maintenance accorded true bonsai.

Adventitious bud – a bud which arises at an unusual place on stem or trunk.

Anneal – to subject to heat and then cool so as to soften thoroughly and render less brittle.

Annuals – plants that complete their growth in a single year.

Axillary bud – a bud borne in an axil, the point at which a leaf stalk or branch diverges from the stem or axis to which it is attached.

Balled-and-burlapped – dug with a ball of soil around the roots, then tied up, pudding fashion, in burlap.

Bare-root – roots without soil.

Cambium – the inner bark that carries the food manufactured in the leaves to the roots.

Cold frame – an unheated, bottomless, boxlike structure with removable top glazed with glass or covered with a translucent material such as plastic.

Collected plants – dug from the countryside (or garden); usually wild or native species, but, in any case, plants which were not started originally as nursery plants in preparation for later transplantation.

Compost – a substitute for manure, made up of a variety of decomposed organic materials or refuse matter, adaptable for use as a fertilizer and as a source of humus.

Conifers – cone-bearing trees such as pines, spruces, cedars, junipers, etc.

Cuttings – pieces of plants without roots which are to be induced to produce roots after they have been cut from the parent plant.

Damping-off – a disease that causes the death of seedlings (and sometimes cuttings) either before they emerge from the soil or during their early days above ground.

Dormant – inactive, or period of winter inactivity.

Genus – a group of species of plants linked together by usually obvious, but sometimes rather puzzling, botanical characteristics.

Grafting – the bringing together of the growing regions (cambium layers) of two different plants under such conditions that they will unite and grow as one.

Ground bed – in bonsai culture, a planting area in the ground, usually used for pre-bonsai training of younger plants, or convalescence for older plants in training.

Hardening, hardening off – the process of making plants ready for outdoors, usually by accustoming them gradually to lower temperatures, less moisture, and to more sunlight and wind.

Hardwood cuttings – pieces taken from a plant after it has finished and ripened its growth, often when it is leafless and dormant.

Heavy soil – soil composed largely of clay.

Humus – decomposed vegetable matter.

Internodes – the intervals or parts between two nodes or joints on a stem or branch.

Layering – propagation of plants by inducing them to form roots on a branch before it is severed from the parent.

Leader – the main trunk or growing apex of a tree.

Leafmold – decayed leaves, woods soil.

Light soil – soil composed largely of sand or granular humus.

Liners – small plants, either grafted, seedlings, or rooted cuttings, suitable for planting in rows in the nursery, or to be grown for another year or two in containers.

Loam – a mixture, in varying proportions, of soil ingredients, from clay to sand, often including some humus.

Naturalized – exotic species which are so well adapted to a region that they may be found growing wild there.

New wood – growth of the current year.

Old wood – ripened wood, of the previous year, or older.

Peat moss – decayed. or partially decayed material from sphagnum-moss bogs or from sedge peat.

Perennials – plants living through more than two seasons of growth, often much more.

Perlite – a white, glasslike silica derivative, about one tenth the weight of sand, useful as medium for rooting cuttings, or as a soil amendment to improve porosity and drainage of a potting mixture.

Pot-bound – a plant with roots so closely packed in the pot that there is little space for further growth.

Scions or scion wood – any bud, shoot, or other portion of a plant for propagation by budding or grafting.

Semihardwood cuttings – cuttings of partially matured new wood, usually taken in early summer.

Slip – a cutting or scion.

Soft-wood cuttings – cuttings taken of new growth, usually in spring.

Species – a group of plants which have in common one or more distinctive characteristics, and do, or may, interbreed and reproduce these characteristics in their offspring.

Sphagnum moss – a peat or bog moss that grows in fresh water, commonly used for packing plants that are to be shipped, and for other horticultural purposes.

Stratification – the process of treating seeds that require a winter season to trigger germination, by mixing the seeds with damp sand and keeping this mixture cold for two months or so.

Sun-pit – a deeper variation of the cold frame, usually large enough for the gardener to enter via steps.

Syringe – to spray the foliage of a plant, to prevent wilting, to encourage growth, or to control certain insects.

Taproot – a primary root which grows downward, giving off lateral rootlets.
Terminal bud – growing at the end of a branch or stem.
Understock, or stock – the rooted plant or part of a plant which is to accept
   the scion in grafting.
Vermiculite – a micalike mineral, much lighter than sand, useful as a medium
   for starting seeds or cuttings.

JAPANESE TERMS

(Some of the many terms used by the Japanese to describe or classify bonsai
are listed here. Pronunciation is similar to Spanish, but without the strong
accenting of certain syllables.)

Back of bonsai – *ura*
Cascade style – *kengai*
    semicascade – *han kengai*
    little fall – *sho kengai*
    medium fall – *chu kengai*
    big fall – *dai kengai*
Front of bonsai – *omote*
Gnarled trunk – *bankan*
Group plantings – *yose ue*
    two trees – *soju*
    three trees – *sambon yose*
    five trees – *nanahon yose*
    seven trees – *shichi hon yose*
    cluster group – *tsukami yose*
    natural group – *yama yori*
    multiple trunked – *kabudachi*
    root-connected – *ne tsuranari*
    several trunks from one trunk – *ikada buki*
Octopus style – *tako zukuri*
One root in pot – *kabu mono*
One tree in pot – *ippon ue*
    single trunk – *tankan*
    double trunk – *sokan*
    three trunks – *sankan*
    five trunks – *gokan*
    seven trunks – *shichikan*
    multiple trunk – *kabudachi*
Raft style, from one root – *ikada buki*
Rock planting – root-over-rock – *seki joju*
    (with roots extending into soil below)
    clinging-to-rock – *ishi tsuki*
    (roots attached to rock)
Roots above ground – *ne agari*
Roots connected – *ne tsuranari*

Size – under 7 inches – *mame bonsai*
    7 to 12 inches – *ko bonsai*
    12 to 26 inches – *chiu bonsai*
    26 to 40 inches or more – *dai bonsai*
    (bonsai are measured from the base of the trunk to the top of the tree, except in the case of cascade types, which are measured from the highest part of the plant to the lowest point of the cascade. All Japanese experts do not agree on these sizes applied to these classifications).
Slanting trunk – *shakan*
Split trunk (or "bark coming off") – *saba miki*
Tokonoma – the shallow alcove in a Japanese home where displays are made for special occasions or the seasons. Here flowers, bonsai, ornamental rocks, or incense burners may be combined with scrolls or calligraphy to honor a guest or to celebrate an event.
Twisted trunk – *nejikan*
Upright – formal style – *chokkan*
    informal, free style – *moyo gi*
Winding-trunked – *kyokkukan*
Wind swept – *fuki na gashi*

BOOKS ON BONSAI

Dwarf Trees by Shinobu Nozaki.
    Tokyo: Sanseido Co., Ltd., 1940
Bonsai—Miniature Potted Trees by Norio Kobayashi.
    Tokyo: Japan Travel Bureau, 1950
Notes on Bonsai by Alfred Koehn.
    Tokyo: Foreign Affairs Ass'n of Japan, 1953
Handbook on Dwarfed Potted Trees, Kan Yashiroda, Editor.
    Brooklyn Botanic Garden, Brooklyn, N.Y. 1953
    (Re-issued 1959)
Bonsai—Miniature Trees by Claude Chidamian.
    New York: D. Van Nostrand Co., Inc., 1955
Bonsai—Photos of Now Famous Miniature Trees, Kenji Murata, Editor.
    Tokyo: Koju-en, Kenji Murata,
    First volume in a series published in 1956
The Art of Growing Miniature Trees, Plants and Landscapes
    by Tatsuo Ishimoto. New York: Crown Publishers, Inc., 1956
The Japanese Art of Miniature Trees and Landscapes
    by Yuji Yoshimura and Giovanna M. Halford.
    Rutland, Vt., and Tokyo: Charles E. Tuttle Co., 1957
Japanese Miniature Trees—Their Style, Culture and Training
    by Kan Yashiroda. Newton, Mass.: C. T. Branford Co., 1960
A Dwarfed Tree Manual for Westerners by Samuel Newsom.
    Tokyo: Tokyo News Service, Ltd., 1960
The Art of Training Plants by Ernesta Drinker Ballard.
    New York: Harper & Brothers, 1962

Index

Abies species. *See* Firs
Acacias (bullhorn), 41
Accessories for display, 99, 106–8
Acer, 66, 185–87. *See also* Maples
A. *buergerianum*, 66, 175, 186, 237
A. *ginnala*, 186
A. *palmatum dissectum*, 49, 66, 175, 186
Aconite, winter, 46
Adapted bonsai, 44, 65–67, 244
Adonis, yellow flowering, 45
Adventitious bud, defined, 244
Aesculus species, 80
African violets, 215
Age, 14–16, 113–22, 159
Air circulation, 211
Air layering, 86–88
Alder, black, 76
American elm, 116, 121
American larch, 234
Amur maple, 186
Anderson, Larz, 35, 37, 234
Andromeda (*Pieris*), 81, 85
  Japanese, 57, 58
Annealed wire, 171, 244
Annuals, defined, 244
Antidessicant spray, 74
Ants, eliminating, 224
Aphids, 223, 224
Apples, 209
  crab, 39, 66, 209
    for color, 46, 50, 51
  seeds, 80
Apricots, 22, 23, 67, 225
  barred from import, 89
  and cold, 39
  grafting, 88
  limiting water for, 209
  pre-bonsai training, 156
  for winter color, 45
Araucaria excelsa, 230, 231
Arborvitae, 82, 85
Arctostaphylos manzanita, 76
Ardisia, 46
Arenarias, 100
Arizona cypress, 76
Arnold Arboretum, 35, 37, 234
Ashes as fertilizer, 146, 217

Atlas cedar, 66
  blue, 40
Australian pine, 67
Autumn display, recommendations for, 46, 50–52
Avery, George S., Jr., 33, 36 n
Axillary bud, defined, 244
Azakusa Park, 23
Azaleas, 66, 187–88, 211, 235
  for color, 46, 48, 49, 50, 51
  from cuttings, 81, 85
  importing, 90
  limited feeding of, 217
  pest control, 224
  wood ashes for, 146

Backgrounds for display, 99, 106–8
Bald cypress, 76, 115, 121, 197–98
  importing, 90
  training, 163
Balled-and-burlapped treatment, 56, 151–53, 244
Balsam fir, 76, 234
Bamboo plants, 26, 67
  barred from import, 89
Bambusa multiplex, 67
Banyan trees, 120
  Chinese, 67
Barbados cherry, 196
Barberries, 66
  for color, 50
  propagation of, 80, 81, 85
  rabbits and, 225
Bare-root treatment, 56, 244
Bark, effects of wiring on, 164, 168
Beeches, 76, 80, 90
  European, 66
Bellflower, Chinese, 46
Berberis (barberry), 50, 66, 225
  propagation of, 80, 81, 85
B. *thunbergi*, 66
B. *verruculosa*, 66
Bermuda juniper, 67
Berried plants. *See also* specific plants
  for autumn color, 50
Betula (birch), 76, 90
B. *papyrifera*, 76

B. populifolia, 76
Big tree redwood, 121
Birches, 76, 90
Birds, damage by, 225
Bishop pine, 77
Bittersweet, 50
Black alder, 76
Black gum, 76
Black pine, 67, 196
    grafting, 88
Black spruce, 234
"Bleeding" sap, 158
Blood meal as fertilizer, 146, 147
Blue atlas cedar, 40
Blue spruce, 85, 234
Bone meal as fertilizer, 146, 147
Books on bonsai, 247–48
Boston, Mass., 35, 37, 234
Boston ivy, 85
Bougainvillea, 67
Boxwood, 66
    cuttings, 85
    importing, 90
Braces for wiring trees, 172
Branches,
    growth and character, 117–22 ff, 127 ff
    training of, 133, 134, 135, 159–70
Brassaia, 67
Bristlecone pine, 25, 114, 120
Brooklyn Botanic Garden, 33–35, 36, 205, 206, 234
    demonstrations of bonsai training, 57–63
Buckeye, 8-o
Budding, 88, 89
Buds, 117, 120, 121, 122
    adventitious, defined, 244
    axillary, defined, 244
    in pines, 206–8
    and pruning, 160, 161, 162, 163, 206–8
    terminal, 117, 246
    and wiring, 160
Bullhorn, 41
Bush clover, 46
Buxus (boxwood), 66, 85, 90
B. microphylla, 66

California juniper, 71
California live oak, 77
California Museum of Science and Industry, 33, 34
California wild lilac, 76
Calliandra surinaemensis, 80
Calomondin, 67
Cambium layer, 244
    growth at, 117
Camellia hiemalis, 52, 67

C. sasanqua, 52, 67
Camellias, 67
    for fall color, 52
    in greenhouses, 235
    and limited feeding, 217
    and pesticide, 224
Canadian hemlock (*Tsuga canadensis*), 75, 76
Carissa, 67
Carpinus (hornbeams), 50, 90, 234
C. caroliniana, 76
Carrington, Richard, 15 n
Cascade-type plants, 128, 176, 179–80
    bases for containers, 106
    containers, 93, 96
    Japanese terms for, 246
    potting, 150
Casuarina equisetifolia, 67
Ceanothus, 76
Cedars, 46, 114
    atlas, 40, 66
    deodar, 66
    incense (*Libocedrus*), 76
    Japanese. See Cryptomeria; False cypress
    red (*Juniperus*), 76, 122
    white (*Chamaecyparis, Libocedrus*), 76
Cedrus species, 66. See also Cedars
Celtis orientalis, 205
Cement for base, 177
Cercis species. See also Redbuds
C. canadensis, 76
C. occidentalis, 77
Chaenomeles (flowering quince), 66, 188. See also Quinces
    for color, 48, 50
    importing, 90
    seeds, 80
C. japonica, 48
C. japonica maulei, 188
Chamaecyparis (false cypress), 66, 81, 90 162
C. Lawsoniana, 76
C. nootkatensis, 76
C. obtusa (Hinoki cypress), 66, 234
C. pisifera, 66
C. thyoides, 76
Cherries, 23, 80, 234
    Barbados, 196
Chestnuts, 80
Children, damage by, 225
Chilopsis linearis, 76
Chinaberry (*Melia*), 80, 174
Chinese banyan, 67
Chinese bellflower, 46
Chinese hackberry, 205
Chinese ixora, 67
Chinese parasol tree, 80, 181, 233
Chrysanthemums, 81, 179

Citron, fingered, 50
Citrus, 67, 231, 235
  pesticides and, 224
  seeds, 78, 80
C. medica, 50
Clamps for wiring trees, 172
Clay, 137–38
  to cover roots, 178
  in potting soil, 139, 140–41, 142, 143, 148
  subsoil, 142, 148
Cleft grafting, 89
Climate, 226–42
  growth pattern and weather, 121–22
Clover bush, 46
Cluster plantings, 174
Coe, Ernest F., 205, 206
Cold frame, 244
Collected plants, 56, 68–77, 244
  mosses, 100–2
  training of, 134
  transplanting of, 154–55
Color,
  collections for, 45–52
  containers and, 93, 95
Colorado spruce, 66
Comfort, Alex, 15 n
Compost, 147–48, 244
Conifers, 244. *See also* Pines
  containers for, 93
  cuttings of, 81
  pruning, 163, 205–8
Container-grown plants, 56–57. *See also* Nursery-grown plants
Containers, 92–98, 133–34, 149–50. *See also* Potting
Contorted willow, Hankow, 42
Cordyline terminalis, 77
Cotoneaster, 66, 129
  for autumn color, 50
  propagation of, 80, 81
Cottonseed meal as fertilizer, 146, 147, 217
Crab apples, 39, 66
  for color, 46, 50, 51
  pruning of, 209
  seeds of, 80
Crape myrtle, 67, 199–200
  cuttings, 82, 85
  midseason repotting, 194
  for summer color, 50
  wiring, 169, 200
Crassula varieties, 230
Crataegus species. *See* Hawthorns
Cryptomeria, importing, 66, 162, 208
  importing, 90
  propagation, 80, 85
C. japonica, 66

Cupressus arizonica, 76
C. funebris, 67
Cuttings, 55, 80–85, 244
  after rooting, 155, 157
  damping-off, 215
  various types, defined, 244, 245
Cycad, 67
Cycas revoluta, 67
Cyperus alternifolius gracilis, 67
Cypresses, 76
  Arizona, 76
  bald, 76, 115, 121, 197–98
    importing, 90
    training, 163
  false, 66, 81, 90, 162
  Hinoki, 66, 234
  Lawson, 76
  Monterey, 111
  mourning, 67
  pond, 76, 179, 197–98
    illustrated, 143

Damping-off, 215, 244
Daphne, 81
Dawn redwood, 66, 85, 198
Deciduous plants. *See also* Potting; Pruning; specific plants
  containers for, 93
  growth pattern, 119–20
  importing, 90
  soil for, 146, 148
  training, 160, 163, 175, 208
Delonix regia, 67
Denver, Colo., bonsai exhibit, 33
Deodar cedar, 66
Desert willow, 76
Diseases, 214–15, 223–25. *See also* Injury, and growth
Displaying bonsai, 26
  accessories, mosses, rocks for, 99–108
  color in, 47–52
  containers as frames for, 92–98
Dogwood, 80
"Dormant," defined, 244
Douglas fir, 76
Drainage, 94, 96–98, 149–50
  potting soil and, 142, 143, 214
Dried manures, 141, 146, 147, 217
Dwarf flowering quince, 48, 188
Dwarf geraniums, 49
Dwarf hollies, 60–65, 66, 189, 231
Dwarf Japanese (flowering) quince, 48, 188
Dwarf mandarin peach, 44
Dwarf Mugo pine, 63
Dwarf sand myrtle, 76
Dwarf Trees, 15 n

Dwarf varieties. *See also* specific plants
  training of, 162
Dwarfed plants, in nature, 163

Eastern hemlock (*Tsuga canadensis*), 75, 76
Elephants, age of, 15
Elephants (Carrington), 15 n
Elms, 116, 121, 181
  seeds of, 80
Emergency treatment for plants, 212
Engelmann's spruce, 123
Epoxy glue, 177
English ivy, 85
Eugenia, 67
Eugenia malaccensis, 77
E. uniflora, 67
Euonymus, 67
European beech, 66
Evergreens. *See also* specific plants
  balled-and-burlapped, 56
  containers for, 93
  growth pattern, 119–20, 208
  importing, 89, 90
  shape of, 116
  soil for, 148
  training, 160, 175, 186

Fagus grandifolia, 76, 80, 90
F. sylvatica, 66
Fall color, plants for, 46, 50–52
False cypress, 66, 162
  cuttings of, 81
  importing, 90
Farkleberry. *See* Sparkleberry
Feather rock, 177
Feeding of plants. *See* Fertilizer (and plant feeding)
Feijoa calleianum, 67
Ferguson, C. W., quoted, 16 n
Fertilizer (and plant feeding), 142, 145–48, 210, 215–17
  for *mame* bonsai, 184, 217
  for very young plants, 157
  and wiring, 166
Ficus diversifolia, 49, 230
F. retusa, 67
Fig, mistletoe, 49, 230
Fingered citron, 50
Fire thorn (*Pyracantha*), 67
  for fall color, 50
  importing, 90
  propagation, 80, 81, 85
Firmiana simplex, 81, 181, 233
Firs, 76, 234
  cuttings of, 85
  growth pattern, 121
  shape when young, 114

Floral sprays, 224
Flowering adonis, yellow, 45
Flowering apricot. *See* Apricots
Flowering cherry, 23, 80, 234
Flowering peach, 80
Flowering plants. *See also* specific plants
  for fall color, 52
  fertilizing, 146, 148, 217
  limited watering, 209
  repotting, 220
  size of blossoms, 126
Flowering quince. *See Chaenomeles*
Foliage. *See* Color: collections for; Leaves
Form, in plant selection, 128–32
Fruiting plants. *See also* specific plants
  berries for fall color, 50
  fertilizing, 146, 148, 217
  repotting, 220
  size of fruits, 126

Gentian, 46
Genus, defined, 244
Geraniums, dwarf, 49
Ginkgo (gingko), 46, 50, 66, 80
  importing, 90
  propagation, 80, 85
Glazed pots, 93, 95, 96
  for *mame* bonsai, 93, 94, 181
Glossary, 244–46
Glue, epoxy, 177
Golden cup oak, 71, 77
Golden larch, 67
Golden raintree (*Koelreuteria*), 85, 174
Grafting, 55, 88–89, 244
Grapevines, 158
Grass bonsai, 46
Gravel, 106
Gray birch, 76
Greene, Harry Ashland, quoted, 16 n
Greenhouses, 231, 234–35
Grevellia robusta, 80
Ground, plants in, 133
  "ground bed," 134, 212, 244
Groups, 173–75
  Japanese terms for, 246
Groves, 173–75, 176, 232
Growth, 114–22. *See also* Training
  limiting, 202–12. *See also* Pruning
Guavas, 67
Gum trees,
  black, 76
  sour, 76
  sweet, 50, 76

Hackberry, Chinese, 205
Hall of Flowers (San Francisco), 3
Hankow contorted willow, 42

Hardening, defined, 244
Hardwood cuttings, defined, 245
Haw, possum (*Ilex decidua*), 76, 189
Hawaii, plants for, 67, 77, 229, 230
Hawthorns, 66, 76
  for autumn color, 50
  importing, 90
  seeds of, 80
Heavy soil. *See also* Clay
  defined, 245
Hemlock, 75, 76, 229, 234
  importing, 90
  propagation, 80, 85
  shape when young, 114
Herb bonsai, 26
Hernandez, Francisco, 41
Hickory, 114
Hinoki cypress, 66, 234
Hollies, 66, 76, 188–89
  dwarf, 60–65, 66, 189, 231
  for indoor use, 231
  Japanese, 60–65, 85, 189, 231
  propagation, 78, 80, 85
  rabbits and, 225
  Siebold, 188–89, 190
Hornbeams, 76, 234
  for autumn color, 50
  importing, 90
Horticultural School (Tokyo), 23
Houseplants, 229–31
Humidity. *See also* Climate; Mist propagation
  adding to, 231, 238
Humus, 138, 139, 147, 244
  as basic ingredient, 141, 142
  possible combinations with, 145

Ibota privet, 72
Iemitsu (shogun), 23
Ilex, 66, 76, 188–89
  I. crenata (Japanese holly), 60–65, 189, 231
  I. crenata helleri, 189
  I decidua, 76, 189
  I. serrata (Siebold holly), 188–89, 190
  I verticillata, 76
  I. vomitoria, 76
Imperial Garden (Tokyo), 23
Importing bonsai, 89–91, 95
Incense cedar, 76
Indoor greenhouses, 231
Indoor plants, 229–31
Injury, and growth, 119–20, 121–22, 123, 125. *See also* Diseases
  wiring and, 168–70
Insecticidal sprays, 223–24
Insects, 223–24

Internodes, defined, 245
Irish moss, 100
Iron rods for wiring trees, 172
Ironwood,
  Casuarina equisetifolia, 67
  Metrosideros collina, 77
  Ostrya virginiana, 76
Ivy, 85
Ixora coccinea, 67

Jacaranda acutifolia, 80, 174
Jack pine, 76
Jade plant, 230
Japan, 22–30. *See also* Potting; Pruning; Selection of plants
  accessories in, 106–8
  climate in, 226–29
  importing bonsai from, 89–91
  rocks in, 102–6
Japan Bonsai Commercial Association, 29
Japan Bonsai Trading Co., Ltd., 29
Japanese andromeda, 57–60
Japanese apricot. *See* Apricots
Japanese barberry, 66
Japanese black pine. *See* Black pine
Japanese cedar. *Sdee* Cryptomeria; False cypress
Japanese holly, 85, 189
  dwarf, 60–65, 189, 231
Japanese maples, 66, 186, 234
  for spring color, 49
Japanese quince. *See* Chaenomeles
Japanese red pine, 23, 196
Japanese terms, 246–47
Japanese white pine, 65, 196
  illustrated, 36, 204
Jasmine, 66, 81
  importing, 90
Jasminum (jasmine), 66, 81, 90
Junipers, 65, 66, 67, 76, 189–94, 234
  growth, 162, 190
  illustrated, 40, 71, 183, 192–93, 227, 240
  importing, 90
  mame, 183
  propagation, 80, 85
  pruning, 190, 208
  for Southwest, 242
Juniperus, 66, 67, 76, 189–94 *See also* Junipers
  J. barbadensis, 67
  J. californica, 71
  J. chinensis sargentii (Sargent juniper), 65, 67, 192
  J. chinensis torulosa, 67
  J. virginiana, 76, 122

Knothole moss, 101
Koelreuteria (Golden raintree), 85, 174
Kumquat, 67

Lagerstroemia indica. See Crape myrtle
"Landscape" stone, 106
Lantana, 194–95
  pruning, 222–23
  for summer color, 49, 50
Lantana camara, 194–95
Larches, 66, 76, 234
  color of, 50
  golden, 67
  planting on rock, 102–5
  seeds, 80
  training, 163
Larix, 66. See also Larches
L. laricina, 76
Laurel, mountain, 85
Lawson cypress, 76
Layering, 55, 85–88, 155, 157
  defined, 245
Leader, defined, 245
Leaf scorch, 186
Leafmold, 147, 245
Leaves,
  and color. See color: collections for
  compound, 174
  and growth of trees, 117 ff
  and pruning, 161–62, 163, 186, 208–9
  reducing size of, 181, 208–9
  scorching of, 186
  on seedlings, 114
  and selection of trees, 123, 125, 126
  and watering, 212, 213, 214
Lehua, 77
Leiophyllum, 76
L. lyoni, 76
Leucaena glauca, 80
Libocedrus decurrens, 76
Light, and growth, 210–11, 212
Light soil, defined, 245
Lighting, for display, 106, 108
Ligustrum (privet), 66, 85
L. obtusifolium, 72
Lilac, 76
Linden, 80
Liners, 64, 245
Liquidambar styraciflua, 50, 76
Live oaks, 77, 111
Loam, 138, 142, 145, 148
  defined, 245
Los Angeles, Calif., bonsai exhibit, 3
Locust, cuttings of, 85

Malpighia, 49, 50, 196
M. coccigera, 50, 51, 196
M. glabra, 196

Malus species. See Apples
Mame bonsai, 27, 180–84, 196
  containers for, 93, 94, 181
  display of, 107
  feeding of, 184, 211
  repotting of, 184, 220
Mandarin peach, dwarf, 44
Manures, 141, 146, 147, 217
Manzanita, 76
Maples, 125, 128, 161, 185–87
  barred from import, 89
  grove of, 232
  and knothole moss, 101
  Japanese, 66, 186, 234
    for color, 49
  propagation of, 78, 80
  shape when young, 114
  for spring color, 49, 50
  sugar, 158
  trident, 66, 186, 237
    on rocks, 175
  wiring of, 168–69, 186
Meiji, Emperor, 23
Melia, 174
M. azedarach, 80
Mesquite, 76
Metasequoia, 66, 85, 198
Metrosideros collina, 77
Mice, damage by, 225
Microclimates, 232–36
Mildew, 223
Mimosa, 174
  cuttings, 85
Miniature bonsai. See Mame bonsai
Mist propagation, 84, 85, 215
Mistletoe fig, 49, 230
Mites, spider, 223, 224
Moisture. See Climate; Watering
Mold, sooty, 224–25
Monterey cypress, 111
Moss, 99–102, 131, 175, 178. See also
    Peat moss; Sphagnum moss
Mountain laurel cuttings, 85
Mountain pine (Pinus virginiana), 69, 76
Mourning cypress, 67
Mugo pine, 63, 67
Mulberry, white, 181
Myrtles,
  crape. See Crape myrtle
  sand, 76
  wax, 85

Naka, John, 71
Nandina, 46
Natural soils, 137–39
Naturalized species, defined, 245
New wood, defined, 245

New York, N.Y., bonsai exhibits, 33. *See also* Brooklyn Botanic Garden
Nitrogen, 145–46
Nootka cypress, 76
Norfolk Island pine, 230, 231
Norway spruce, 66
Nozaki, Shinobu, 15 n, 27
Number of trunks on multiple plantings, 173
Numbers, plant selection and, 125
Nursery-grown plants, 55, 56–67, 129–32, 134, 135, 152–54
  pot sizes for, 96
  special problems, 153–54
Nyssa aquatica, 76
N. sylvatica, 76

Oaks, 80, 112, 114
  golden cup, 71, 77
  live, 77, 111
  scrub, 77
  silk, 80
Ohelo, 77
Ohia, 77
Okamura, Frank, 57–60
Old wood, defined, 245
Olea, 39, 67
Olive, 39, 67
Organic fertilizers, 146–48, 217. *See also* Manures
Ostrya virginiana, 76

Palm, sago, 67
Parasol tree, 80, 181, 233
Peaches, 50, 80, 209
  dwarf mandarin, 44
Pears, 50, 209
Peat moss, 83, 141, 147, 245
Pebbles, 102, 106
Pepperidge, 76
Perennials, defined, 245
Perlite, 83, 245
Persimmon, 46
Pests, 223–25, 229
Phosphate, 145–46
Photographs, for planning bonsai, 128–29
Picea, 66, 76, 77. *See also* Spruces
P. abies, 66
P. pungens, 66
Pieris, 81, 85
P. japonica, 57, 58
Pineapple guava, 67
Pines, 65, 67, 76, 227, 235
  Australian, 67
  bishop, 77
  black, 67, 88, 196
  bristlecone, 25, 114, 120
  collecting, 74

for color, 45, 50
containers for, 93
displayed in Japan, 23
and feeding, 197, 217
illustrated, 38, 39, 206–8. *See also* specific species
jack, 76
and junipers contrasted, 189–90
mountain (*Pinus virginiana*), 69, 76
Mugo, 63–64, 67
pinion, 77, 228
pitch, 76, 234
potting soil, 148, 196–97
propagation, 80, 85, 88, 89
and pruning, 158, 160, 162, 163, 197, 205–8
  of Mugo pine, 63–64
red, 23, 196
repotting, 197, 220
scrub, 76
shore, 77
for Southwest, 242
"spruce." *See Tsuga canadensis*
and sunshine, 197, 211
Torrey, 122
white, 23, 65, 88, 196
  illustrated, 36, 204
wiring, 158, 197
Pinion pine, 77, 228
Pinus, 67, 76. *See also* Pines
P. banksiana, 76
P. cembroides (Pinion pine), 77, 228
P. contorta, 77
P. densiflora, (Japanese red pine), 23, 196,
P. echinata, 76
P. Mugo (Mugo pine), 63, 67
P. muricata, 77
P. parviflora, (Japanese white pine), 65, 196
  illustrated, 36, 204
P. rigida (pitch pine), 76, 234
P. sylvestris, 67
P. thunbergii. See Black pines
P. Virginiana, 69, 76
Pistachio (*Pistacia*), 47, 49, 50, 174
Pistacia. See Pistachio
Pitch pine, 76, 234
Pittosporum, 67
Plastic, uses for, 74, 79, 83, 87
Poinciana, royal, 67
Pomegranates, 50, 67, 211
  cuttings of, 82
  importing, 90
  for indoor use, 231
Pond cypress, 76, 179, 197–98
  illustrated, 143
Port Orford cedar, 76

Possum haw (*Ilex decidua*), 76, 189
Potash, 146
"Pot-bound," defined, 245
Pots, 92–98, 133–34, 149–50. *See also*
    Potting
Potting, 149–57
  repotting, 194, 217–23
  soil for, 136–49, 150, 153, 214
Privet, 66, 85
  Ibota, 72
Prosopis, 76
Pruning, 117, 152, 158–63, 202–9
  leaf, 161–62, 186, 208–9
  natural, 119, 120
  results shown, 129–32, 157, 159, 218–
    19
  root, 134, 151, 157, 158, 203, 217–23
  scars, 125
Prunus. See also various flowering fruit
    trees
  P. "Hally Jolivette," 50
  P. *mume. See* Apricots
Pseudolarix amabilis, 67
Pseudotsuga, 76
Psidium cattleianum, 67
Pukiawe, 77
Punica. See Pomegranates
Pyracantha (fire thorn), 67
  for fall color, 50
  importing, 90
  P. *coccinea*, 67
  propagation, 80, 81, 85

Quercus species. *See also* Oaks
Q. agrifolia (live oak), 77, 111
Q. chrysolepsis, 71, 77
Q. dumosa, 77
Quinces, 66, 188
  for color, 48, 50
  fruit on, 180, 183
  importing, 90
  propagation, 80, 82

Rabbits, damage by, 225
Raintree, golden, 85
Raker, James R., 127, 129
Rape cake as fertilizer, 146
Red cedar, 76, 122
Red pine, Japanese, 23, 196
Red spruce, 234
Redbud, 50, 76, 77
  cuttings, 85
Red-leaf barberry, 50
Redwood, 39, 66, 121
  dawn, 66, 85, 198
Reindeer moss, 100
Rhododendron, 146. *See also* Azaleas
Rhododendrons, 146

Rocks, 99, 102–6, 175–79
  Japanese terms, 247
  in training roots, 154, 177–79
  for "triangle," 124
Rohdeas, 50
Rooting of cuttings. *See* Cuttings
Roots, 114–15, 119
  ground bed and, 133
  pruning, 134, 151, 157, 158, 203, 217–
    23
  for rock arrangements, 175, 178
  and selection of trees, 123, 127
  and soil, 138, 143, 145
  training, 150, 154, 178
Royal poinciana, 67

Sago palm, 67
Salix species. *See also* Willows
S. *matsudana toruosa*, 42
San Francisco, Calif., bonsai exhibit, 3
Sand, 136 ff, 157
Sand myrtle, 76
Sap, 166
  bleeding, 158
Sargent juniper (*Juniperus chinensis sar-
    gentii*), 65, 67, 192
Sawara cypress, 66
Scale insects, 224
Scotch pine, 67
Screens for display, 108
Scions, defined, 245
Scrub oak, 77
Scrub pine, 76
Seasonal displays, 45–52
Seedlings, 155, 157 *See also* Seeds
  in clusters, 174
  damping-off, 215
  pruning, 163
  root training for special needs, 178
Seeds, 55, 78–80
Selection of plants, guidelines for, 110–
    28
Semihardwood cuttings, 245
Shade, 211, 212, 236
Shishi-gashira, 52, 67
Shore pine, 77
Shrubs. *See also* specific plants
  growth pattern of, 120
  training, 160
Siebold, Karl Theodor Ernst von, 26
Siebold holly, 188–89, 190
Sieving of soil, 139–41
Silk oak, 80
Silt, 142
Sitka cypress, 76
Size, Japanese terms for, 247
Sketches, in planning bonsai, 128–29
Slanting style, 124, 128, 179

Slender umbrella plant, 67
Slip, defined, 245
Soft-wood cuttings, 245
Soil, 136–49, 230. *See also* Fertilizer;
  Watering; specific plants
  natural, 137–39
  original, for transplanting, 74–75
  for seeds, 79
  substitutes for, 153–54
Sooty mold, 224–25
Sophora, 80
Sour gum, 76
South, species favored in, 67. *See also*
  Climate
Southwest, species favored in, 67. *See also*
  Climate
Spanish moss, 100
Sparkleberry, 69, 70, 76
Species, defined, 245
Sphagnum moss, 84, 87, 100, 147, 178
  defined, 245
Spider mites, 223, 224
Splints for wiring trees, 172
Spraying,
  antidesiccant, 74
  insecticidal, 223–24
  mist propagation, 84, 85, 215
  to water plants, 209–10, 212, 223, 238
Spring display, recommendations for, 46,
  50
"Spruce pine." *See Tsuga canadensis*
Spruces, 25, 65, 66, 76, 77, 234, 239
  barred from import, 89
  for fall color, 46
  propagation, 80, 85
  with rocks, 178
  shapes, 114, 121, 123
Stock, defined, 246
Stone chips, 106
Stones. *See* Rocks
Storms, tree growth and, 121–22
Stratification, 79, 80, 245
Strawberry guava, 67
String,
  for transplanting, 150–51
  for wiring, 172
Styphelia tameiameiae, 77
Subsoil, 142, 148
Sumach, 50
Summer display, recommendations for, 46,
  50
Sun-pit, 233, 245
Swamp cypress. *See* Bald cypress
Sweet gum, 50, 76
Sweetflag, 46
Sycamore, 114
Syringing, 209–10
  defined, 246

Tamarack, 76
Tamarisk (*tamarix*), 67
  cuttings, 85
  importing, 90
  repotting, 194
  training, 130–32, 211
Tamarix. See Tamarisk
Taproots, 114–15, 119, 155, 246
Taxodium ascendens (pond cypress), 76,
  179, 197–98
  illustrated, 143
T. distichum (bald cypress), 76, 115, 121,
  197–98
  importing, 90
  training, 163
Taxus (yew), 67, 80, 85
Terminal buds, 117, 246
Ti plant, 77
Tokonoma, 26, 27, 45, 247
Tokyo, 23
Tools,
  for collecting wild plants, 73
  for cuttings, 83
  for pruning, 158–59
  for wiring, 170–72
Topsoils, 142, 148
Torrey pine, 122
Training, 158–72. *See also* Pruning,
  Wiring
  diet in, 145
  pots, 98
Transplanting. *See* Collected plants; Nurs-
  ery-grown plants; Potting
Triangle, the, 28, 124
Trident maples, 66, 186, 237
  on rocks, 175
Trunks,
  growth and character, 117–28 *passim*,
  133
  in natural dwarfs, 163
  training, 134, 159, 163–70
Tsuga species, 76, 90. *See also* Hemlock
T. canadensis, 75, 76
T. caroliniana, 76
T. heterophylla, 76
Tupelo, 76
Turnbuckles, in wiring trees, 172

Ueno Park (Tokyo), 27
Umbrella plant, 67
Understock, defined, 246

Vaccinium arboreum (sparkleberry), 69,
  70, 76
V. reticulatum, 77
Vermiculite, 83, 245

Walls as backgrounds for display, 108
Warty barberry, 66
Water sprouts, 120
Watering, 150, 213–15. *See also* Drainage; Mist propagation
  adding to, 231, 238
  emergency, 212
  limiting of, 209–10
  of *mame* bonsai, 181–84
Wax myrtle cuttings, 85
Weather, 121–22
  adapting bonsai to climate, 226–42
West Coast, species favored in, 67. *See also* Climate
Western hemlock, 76
Western redbud, 77
White birch, 76
White cedars, 76
White mulberry, 181
White pines, 23, 65, 196
  grafting, 88
  illustrated, 36, 204
White spruce, 234
Wild lilac, California, 76
Wild plants. *See* Collected plants
Willows, 42, 76
  propagation, 82, 85
  pruning, 222–23
  repotting, 194
Wind-swept styles, 128, 179, 211

Winter aconite, 46
Winter display, recommendations for, 45
Wiring, 129, 130, 131, 158, 163–72
  to stabilize plants, 150, 154, 178
Wistaria. See Wisteria
Wisteria, 23, 199, 200
  cuttings of, 82
  importing, 90
Wood ashes as fertilizer, 146, 217
Wood for display, 106–7
Wooden boxes for training, 133
Wright, Frank Lloyd, 106

Yaupon, 76
Yeddo spruce, 25, 65, 89
Yellow cypress, 76
Yellow flowering adonis, 45
Yew, 67, 80, 85
Yoshido, Kenko, quoted, 22
Young Men's Bonsai Association, 29
Young plants, 155–57. *See also* Cuttings; Growth; Seedlings
  pruning, 162–63

Zelkova (*Zelkova serrata*), 67, 116, 121, 234
  importing, 90
  leaf pruning, 209
  reduction of leaf size, 181